The Burden of Silence

A Small Town Minister and His Wife Speak Out Against Jim Crow

by David McDonald

Book Production by
Legacy Publishing Services
legacypublishing.services

Book Cover by Adama R. McDonald

ISBN: 9798857155615

David McDonald
burdenofsilence@gmail.com
Sherwood, Arkansas

Table of Contents

Acknowledgments

For me, sitting in front of a computer screen and putting a story together was, in the beginning, a solitary process. However, polishing the manuscript and all the other tasks to get this book to print is a group effort.

Ali Welky provided the first edit. She helped me focus on the strong and weak points that needed work. Not to mention telling me to add or delete commas and to check my spelling and sentence structure. Book Production was handled by Linda K. Carter (wonderwomancreative.com). Linda covered all aspects of putting the book together. Without Linda this book would not be in print.

In the middle of this process, I had to put the book down to care for my parents through the illnesses that ultimately led to their death. There were those who encouraged me to pick up this book again and trudge on. They also added encouragement and suggestions that kept me going. Three of my brothers; Ron, Don and Tom McDonald encouraged me along the way as well as adding stories that I could use. My cousins, John Welch and Phyllis Welch Dacus told me stories and provided pictures from my mother's side of the family. My aunt, Betty Lilly told me stories from my father's side and corrected some of my errors. Adama Rain McDonald designed the book cover.

Sinaed Collins and Margaret O'Mahony provided feedback from Ireland. Looking at the story from another country and culture helped me clarify what needed emphasis.

Then there were those who provided encouragement without even knowing they were doing so. These people would often tell me stories of my parents that motivated me to continue. A partial list of those people are Sharron Lloyd, Belinda Snow, Martha Hampton Carle, Carol Hampton Rasco, Rebecca McDonald, Amy Lee, Dr. Jim Waldron, Leo Sufka, Rev. Jim Clemmons, and Rev. Michael Maddox.

So many people have been a part of this book that I am sure I have left some important people out. For that I am sorry. It takes a village and even though I have missed some of you, I do know you and know the help you provided.

Author's Note

This is a true story. Care has been taken to be accurate. However, much of the book, including the dialogue, has been reconstructed from people's memories of events and knowledge of how the events unfolded decades ago. Some names and identifying information have been changed.

Care has also been taken to explain the culture of the time and the laws (official and unofficial) of Jim Crow accurately. Any mistakes are mine and are my responsibility.

Finally, a few words about the use of the "N" word. It is a terrible word, but because it was used so frequently in those days, I debated long and hard whether it should be used in this story. It speaks to the destructiveness, not only in its common usage, but in the hateful way in which it was thrown around. Rather than spell it out, I settled on, "n*****." There were two exceptions. One time was in a quote in which the word was used in an unusual way and it seemed important to me that the word be clearly understood. The other time was when it was given to an employee to be used as his name. The act of assigning a person that name seemed to me to be so horrible that I hoped that seeing the word in print brought home to the reader the evil inflicted on the man.

Dedication

This book is dedicated to Charles and Lois McDonald, the subjects of this book. They instilled in me a blueprint for living that has served me well throughout my life.

Preface

~

Extraordinary Tale of the Ordinary

It was a beautiful day. The leaves covered the trees in the rich, deep green of late summer. The light breeze felt comfortably cool. The South can be brutally hot and humid, but the dog days had passed and the humidity level and temperature were finally bearable. My parents, Charles and Lois McDonald, had asked me to go with them to look at a retirement home. I followed them as they walked along the shaded pathway lined with Bradford pear trees that led into one of the buildings. They were holding hands. I smiled, thinking of Dad's running joke that they were not being romantic, just practical. They held hands so they wouldn't fall.

This trip was bittersweet. I was honored that they had asked me to go with them, but a retirement home is where old people go to live out their final years and eventually die. I didn't want my parents to die. I didn't even want them to be old.

As I observed my parents, my mind began to wander back to decades past. Dad was a Methodist minister, and Mother was a stay-at-home mom. It was a time when the Civil Rights Movement was changing the South's way of life. Together they shared an uncompromising belief in the equality of all people, and this belief made it impossible to stay silent in this tumultuous time.

They were ordinary people with ordinary problems, but there was a theme throughout their lives: a respect for all people that wasn't the norm in the segregated South I grew up in. It was during those times that I believed my parents were the most courageous people I knew.

Watching Mother and Dad in front of me, I thought of their life's journey. It traversed Michigan, Texas, and Arizona, but mostly it wound through the small towns and villages of Arkansas.

That was when the idea of writing their story first took root.

~ ~ ~

Soon after that late summer day, they were given the opportunity to serve in a United Methodist church in the high desert community of Las Vegas, New Mexico. I argued against them going. Both were struggling with multiple health issues. One day, Dad and I were sitting on the porch and I was listing health problems, citing them as a reason not to go.

He looked at me, smiling, and said, "David, I'm going to live till I die."

I laughed, "Well, that makes sense." Immediately convinced, I joined my parents in preparing for the move.

Mother told me that just the thought of moving was breathing new life into Dad. She didn't admit it, but she was also becoming reinvigorated.

Their time in New Mexico lasted two years. They loved the church, were fascinated with the culture, and lived only a few blocks from my brother Tom, his wife, Junko, and their two daughters, Amy and Maya.

Upon their return to Arkansas, my parents and I embarked on the task of recording the early years of their lives. I would sit, listen, then go home and write. Then I would read the scenes to them on the phone or go by their house and let them correct any mistakes. We caught ourselves reliving the events again and again. It was a wonderful experience, almost as if I were meeting my parents when they were young.

In time, age caught up with them. I finished the work of recording their stories but put aside the manuscript while concentrating on their health. In 2018, at the encouragement of my brother Ron, I resumed the work of putting my parents' stories into a book.

Sometimes, everyday people have extraordinary tales that are hidden in their attics with other relics of their lives. My parents were just such people.

Introduction

~

The End in the Beginning

The alarm jostled me out of my sleep at 6:30 on the morning of September 6, 2012. 'This can't go on much longer,' I thought. I struggled out of bed and into the kitchen. As is my custom, I had not allowed any extra time to prepare for and arrive at work, so I put those thoughts out of mind and hurried through my morning routines. I had an important meeting scheduled, so I dressed in a white shirt with a bright-yellow-and-blue-striped tie, then headed into the office.

Ready and headed to work, I stepped outside to a beautiful late summer morning, with the temperature in the seventies. It would eventually reach the nineties, but we were experiencing a wonderful break from the hundred-degree days that we had sweated through only a few weeks before.

At work, I was preparing for the meeting when the phone rang. It was my niece, Betsy. We had grown close in the past months, and I found her to be a wonderful person. As a nurse, she had the ability to handle difficult situations with the proper mix of detachment and concern.

"I was with Pop all night, and I'm with him now. I don't think it's imminent, but he will probably not make it through the day," Betsy said.

After a stammering start, I told her I had a couple of things to do at work, but as soon as I completed those tasks, I would head over there. I immediately rang Scott, my son.

"Scott, I just heard from Betsy, and she thinks Pop will die soon, probably today."

"Do you think I should go there now?" he asked.

"Probably so." I paused to check my phone. "Betsy is calling me, let me call you back."

"Hello, Betsy."

"He's gone." I often tease Betsy about her inability to cry, and she responds by labeling me a crybaby. This time she was crying. "I'm sorry you weren't here, but it was peaceful. Grandma and I were at his side."

I called Scott and gave him the news, then went into the hallway. I worked with an office of deaf people, interpreters, and people who can sign. Near my office was an interpreter, and as I stopped at her office door to tell her I was leaving, the words wouldn't come.

"My father died," I finally signed.

"I knew it the moment I saw your face," she said out loud, without even signing.

There is no doubt an easy explanation for what happened next, but to me it seemed that several of my colleagues materialized out of thin air. Still not able to talk, I signed that my father had died.

"You need to go immediately," a woman answered back in sign language. A little disoriented, I stood where I was. I think it was three people who hugged me.

"Go," the woman signed. I did.

~ ~ ~

The drive to the assisted care facility was hard for the obvious reason — I had just lost my father. I called one of my

bosses, Dr. Adrienne Robinson, and told her I would not be at the meeting that day and why, then I cried all the way there. As I was getting out of the car and entering the building, my phone beeped – a text message from my niece, Betsy, "I love you."

I met her at the door and whispered, "I love you, too."

My mother, moving quickly for an 84-year-old woman with her own health problems, rushed over to embrace me. "I know you wanted to be here, and I'm sorry you weren't."

"It's okay; I have been here all through this, and that's what's important to me."

Dad was lying in a hospital-style bed in the front room of my parents' two-room, hospice apartment. His eyes were shut, but his month was wide open.

For several hours, the apartment was flooded with people. There was the hospice nurse, Mary, who came to clean Dad's body and record information for his death certificate. We were asked to leave for the short time it would take to prepare his body. As I stepped out of the room, my mind wandered to when we first received the news that no medical procedures or medicines were working and he would soon pass.

Dad was clear with the doctor and his family that he "was not messed up about dying."

One afternoon, Dad calmly asked Betsy what his death would be like. The question came across as a simple curiosity. Without hesitation, Betsy took her grandfather's hand; her speech was gentle, and her love for Dad seemed a physical presence. There were no euphemisms offered nor did she avoid uncomfortable aspects of the descriptions. Betsy told him how he would lose energy and appetite, sleeping more and more. Finally, in all likelihood, he would die in his sleep.

My dad, her grandfather listened without obvious emotions or comment.

"When will I release my bowels?"

"Sometimes it's right before death and sometimes after," Betsy answered.

After contemplating what he had just been told, a familiar smirk came to his face. "I think I would prefer after."

We laughed and drifted into another conversation.

We discussed Dad's death many times, and he indeed "was not messed up" about it. But just because death was a frequent conversation topic didn't mean it was easy.

I found nothing easy about losing someone I loved. What his humor did was to help me and others face the eventual outcome and ease the dread. For that I was grateful.

~ ~ ~

After he died, employees from the assisted care facility came by in surprisingly large numbers, telling stories of how Dad touched their lives. Often, we, the family, comforted the staff. Three individuals, Cullianne, Tameka, and Joy, were able to sit with us and tell us their stories of my father while we regaled them with tales of our own. I cannot come up with the words to express how meaningful those conversations were. These three women had cared for Dad and continued to assist my mother with skill and love.

In short order, family began arriving. Of my parents' six sons, three were near enough to arrive in time to sit with Dad's body. A multitude of grandchildren showed up. My son, Scott, and his ten-year-old daughter, Adama, arrived within an hour of his death. Both had played a major role in Dad's care.

Dad had donated his body to science at Genesis Hospital, a research facility in Memphis, Tennessee. When the vehicle transporting the body arrived, the driver seemed ill at ease. He made little eye contact and kept his eyes downcast, but he moved the body onto the gurney skillfully. All the laughter and joking stopped as we looked at the Reverend Charles Paul McDonald, Jr., for the last time. He had courageously stood in support of civil rights when that stand was unpopular. He was a husband, father, grandfather, and great-grandfather who provided unwavering love and support. He had died just as he wanted — being of service to those around him for as long as he could, with his humor intact to the end, and surrounded by those he loved.

Just as his face was being covered, I asked the man to wait. Walking up to Dad, I placed my hand on his head. He was cold. I kissed him on his forehead.

This was it. The last time I would see his face or speak to him. I doubt if I have ever felt sadness like I was experiencing in that moment. My voice trembled, and I could barely see through the tears. "Thank you, Dad. I love you."

Mother moved to my side. "Do you want to say goodbye?" I asked, hugging her.

"I already have."

The man covered Dad's face and left.

~ ~ ~

This is the story of my parents, Charles and Lois McDonald. Together they spent a lifetime devoted to their faith, their belief in the sacredness of all people, and their steadfast love of their family and friends.

Part One

~

A Growing Conviction

The Beginning ~ Dad

Charles Paul McDonald, Jr.

It wasn't easy for my dad, the college student, to get from Arkansas to Michigan in 1945, but there was a Methodist Youth Conference coming up in Michigan consisting of young people from around the country, and he really wanted to attend.

The United States was still fighting in World War II, and many commodities were being rationed. Even if Charles owned a car, he would not have been able to get the ration cards to buy the needed gas. He could take a bus, but that took money that was as scarce as extra ration cards. So, he took the only choice available to him. He hitchhiked.

Starting early in the morning, he caught a ride with an Arkansas Best Freight truck out of Fort Smith, Arkansas. The driver took him north, far into Missouri. From there, he thumbed several shorter rides, and after a long, exhausting trip, he arrived at the conference.

This trip was in response to a feeling that had been growing inside Charles since high school, when he first felt "called" to the ministry. There was no conversion experience or burning bush; it was simply a sensation that grew stronger as he got older. He was a student at Hendrix College, a small Methodist Church school in Conway, Arkansas, where he was fast-tracking his ministerial education by attending summer school and carrying a heavy academic load. Upon graduation, Charles planned to attend seminary at Southern Methodist University in Dallas, Texas.

At nineteen, Charles was old enough to serve in the military, and he planned to enlist as a chaplain as soon as he completed his studies. This trip was part of what he saw as his education toward his calling. But it was to shape him in ways he never expected, and it started in an unforgettable manner.

~ ~ ~

Charles found signs directing him to the conference, he lugged his suitcase to the building housing the registration desk. There he was told that he had a dorm assignment with another southerner.

"Where's he from?" he asked.

"Texas," said the woman seated behind the desk. "He is in the room. You can meet him."

In a matter of minutes, Charles was hauling his baggage down a dormitory hallway and to his room. He opened the door and found himself face-to-face with a Black man. Never before had he faced a situation remotely similar. In Arkansas, and for that matter in Texas, not only would the two men have been assigned different rooms, they would have been assigned to different buildings. To room together back home would be breaking a time-honored set of laws referred to as Jim Crow, which mandated the separation of the races. Those who ignored the laws faced brutal penalties enforced by fellow citizens, law enforcement agencies, and terrorist organizations such as the Ku Klux Klan (KKK).

"My name is Julius Scott," the man said, extending his hand.

"Charles McDonald." They shook hands as equals.

The nineteen-year-old ministerial student from Arkansas thought of marching back to registration and getting a new room assignment. He hesitated.

"This is a Christian gathering," he thought. "I can't refuse to room with someone because of the color of his skin. That's not Christian."

Charles unpacked his suitcase and settled in.

~ ~ ~

The decision to stay in the Michigan dormitory room put Charles in conflict with a lifetime of teachings. He lived in a white society that believed in the inferiority of "colored" people. His family, his church, and everyone he knew believed Negroes or colored people (the accepted term for Black people at the time) should be relegated to separation from white people and to second-class citizenship. To top it off, these views were not just customs, they were the law. Harsh penalties were dealt out to those who did not follow the laws of segregation.

For generations, his ancestors had accepted and even supported slavery and later segregation. Charles' great-great-grandfather had owned a plantation with slaves in South Carolina. His great-grandfather fought in the Civil War and was wounded, captured, and put in a northern prison camp. Folklore said that he would not say the word "Yankee" without preceding it with the word "damn" or spitting. J.J. Galloway, his grandfather, served as a minister in the small town of Morrilton, Arkansas, in the early part of the twentieth century. He once received a $50 donation from the Ku Klux Klan for his good work. Fifty dollars was a considerable amount of money, and his grandfather was proud of the recognition.

Charles' mother and father also shared the belief that segregation was right and just, and they seemed to have never questioned the separation of the races.

~ ~ ~

Charles Plato McDonald, Sr., was a World War I veteran. He was a quiet man who got along well with people and believed that his word was his bond. He was active in Goddard Memorial Methodist Church in Fort Smith, Arkansas, serving for many years as the superintendent for the Sunday School. He married Evangel Galloway, and they had three children: Mary, then Charles, and finally Betty. Mary was the rule follower, but Charles and Betty were the mischievous ones, sometimes expressing thoughts that were not exactly in line with what they had been taught.

During the Great Depression, Charles Sr. lost his grocery store and eventually ended up a traveling salesman. There were occasions when Charles Jr. accompanied his father on sales calls. Charles, Sr. treated his customers with genuine respect and interest, catching up on their lives before taking their orders. He then made sure the invoice was accurate before promptly calling the wholesaler. Charles Jr. observed this and was strongly influenced by the honesty, integrity, and care his father showed in his dealings with the people on his route.

Evangel Galloway McDonald was as deeply religious as her husband, but she was firm and somewhat harsh in her interpretation of her faith and what she expected of her children.

Not long after World War II, Charles Jr.'s sister Betty began dating a German American young man who was Catholic. Evangel was not disturbed that he was from a country that had been America's enemy, but she disapproved of her daughter dating a Catholic, even though Catholics and Methodists simply followed different denominations of a common faith.

However, Evangel's uncompromising and strict faith also carried an upside. She believed that a person should live with integrity, honesty, and respect for others. Of course, the "others" she felt she should respect were mostly other white people and other Methodists, but her son, Charles, would eventually cause her to question those prejudices. Ironically, his family and his ancestors—those who owned slaves and accepted money from the KKK—were the very people who taught Charles that he should unpack his bags in Michigan and stay with a Black man. He simply expanded the principles he was taught – treating people with honesty and respect – to include more than just those who were white.

Charles Jr. not balking at being assigned a Black roommate, Julius Scott, because Charles thought it would be "the Christian thing to do" was a small step with huge implications.

According to the culture he came from and its laws, Black people were inferior in every way. According to that culture, staying in the same room with Julius Scott was both immoral and unchristian.

During their time in Michigan, the two men ran in different circles, but Charles watched Julius throughout the week. The man was talented, the life of the party, and well respected. In fact, when Charles compared himself to his roommate, he concluded that Julius was the better man of the two. And Charles was just as impressed by what Julius was not: shiftless, lazy, rude, dirty, or dumb. He fit none of the stereotypes that Charles had heard since childhood.

When the conference was over, Charles hitchhiked back to Arkansas with the knowledge that the man he roomed with was his equal in every way.

Arriving home, he told his mother about the trip. "Mother, I stayed with a colored man."

"A colored man?" A shocked Evangel said to her son.

"It's alright, Mother, nothing bad happened," he said, laughing.

In 1945, no one he knew was discussing a different view of race relations. The young Hendrix College student did not even have the basic vocabulary for such a discussion.

Although he did not talk to his mother about what he was thinking, he had left the conference with two shocking thoughts. First: Julius Scott was a man equal to anyone at the conference. Second, a much more radical idea: perhaps the laws that denied Julius Scott an equal place in society were wrong.

These were unsettling views, but a seed was planted. For the first time, Charles began thinking that he might not only have been called by God to be a minister. He could have also been called to speak out against the injustice of racism.

~ ~ ~

By the time Charles graduated from Hendrix College, World War II had ended, so he enrolled in Perkins School of Theology at Southern Methodist University (SMU) in Dallas, Texas. He and three other seminary students rented an apartment, and unknowingly each person brought into the living arrangement a willingness to discuss the issue of race.

Jim Workman, another Arkansan, came from a family that had opposed segregation and racism for years. During World

War II, while living in Chicago, Jim's parents had hired a Japanese man to be their gardener so he could avoid being sent to one of the concentration camps where Japanese Americans were being placed. It was only after the war that the Workman family learned that the gardener they harbored was, in reality, a Ph.D. scientist.

Clarence Snelling was from New Orleans, Louisiana. He was a person with a disability and was the victim of discrimination himself. While in college, Clarence announced his engagement to a young woman who was a fellow student. When he met his fiancée's parents, they immediately pulled her out of school and warned Clarence to stay away. The young woman's father told Clarence that his daughter would not marry a "cripple."

The next roommate was Mike Patison from Fort Worth, Texas. Mike brought an attitude of openness and a desire to see a just and fair society.

Finally, Charles brought to the table his experience with Julius Scott.

While juggling the responsibilities of school, a social life, and the jobs they took to help pay for seminary, the four friends talked, sometimes into the wee hours of the morning. A frequent topic was race. In those discussions, they concluded that any laws that defined a group as inferior and denied those people equal rights were wrong and should be eliminated.

Expressing his young leanings toward equality, Charles joined with others from SMU and petitioned the school to allow Black and Jewish students to attend classes at the seminary. He also became a lifeguard for a YMCA facility that catered to Hispanic kids.

At SMU, the seed that was planted at the youth conference in Michigan began to grow. These new and radical beliefs were not yet fully formed, but they were early lessons for his life in service to his faith.

The Beginning ~ Mother

Lois Lee King McDonald

Lois Lee King was the daughter of Chester Thaddeus King, a colorful, headstrong fellow also known as Check, or C.T. Her mother was Beulah Irene Clibourn King. Check hated his middle name so much that he was willing to fight anyone who dared to address him as Chester Thaddeus. Check enjoyed a good yarn, and several of his stories were passed down through the years. It is almost certain that the events in the stories took place, but the details may have veered to the left or right of reality.

Long before leaving home, it was clear that he was destined for a life in the business world. As a teenager, he built and operated a moonshine still. Because he was gone from home for long periods of time with no legitimate excuse and because he had money he could not account for, his father, J.D. King, suspected his son was manufacturing and selling 'shine. He was right. Check had located a small plot of land that was isolated and not easily accessible, and J.D. couldn't catch him or find the still.

On a day when Check decided to walk rather than take the time to saddle up his horse, J.D. found his chance. The young man's father waited patiently until Check had a good head start then saddled and mounted Check's horse. He then let go of the reins, allowing the horse to lead him straight to his son's still. Not hearing the rider and horse approach until the last minute, Check only had time to dive behind a log. The animal stopped and Check looked up into the stern face of his father sitting on the horse.

"Hello," Check said, feeling every bit as foolish as he looked.

"Whatcha doing here, Check?"

"Just takin' a nap."

J.D. was rendered temporarily speechless while he contemplated his son's explanation and the fully operational still spread out in front of him.

After Check stood and brushed off the clinging leaves and dirt, J.D. said, "Guess I'll have to tell your momma about it."

That particular threat meant punishment no teenager was interested in enduring.

Check protested, "No, Daddy, please don't tell Momma."

It seemed an eternity before Check's father uttered his fateful decision.

"I won't *if* you will destroy the still and promise me you won't do this no more."

"I promise, Daddy. I promise."

Not wanting to give his father any time to reconsider his decision, Check went to work dismantling what only a few minutes earlier he had viewed as a masterpiece. Thus, the ambitious teenager's first entrepreneurial venture ended in failure.

Check went on to several jobs. There was construction work, breaking horses, and farm work. At twenty-one years old, while working at a rock quarry and living in a tent, he met a sixteen-year-old girl by the name of Beulah Irene Clibourn. They courted then married, and in short order they had a baby boy. They named him Chester Thaddeus King, Jr., ironically the same name Check despised.

~ ~ ~

All was not well on the home front. Arkansas was a poor state. Jobs were scarce and wages low. It wasn't easy to raise a family on the amount of money Check brought home.

He was also having a hard time getting along with his mother-in-law, 'Mama Clibourn.' Beulah was close to her mother — Check thought too close. He saw her as a mama's girl, and he was probably correct. Beulah was, by then, only seventeen, and she depended on her mother for guidance in most areas of her life. Beulah's mother was as headstrong as Check, and his complaints did nothing to decrease her domination of Beulah.

At this stage of our story, two different narratives of Check and Beulah's tale emerge. One is that jobs were hard to come by and Check believed that if he were going to make a good living, he would have to leave Arkansas. The other version is that Check wanted to get out of the reach of his mother-in-law. Maybe it was a little of both. The year was 1927, and he made the announcement that the King family was moving west.

The young man wasted little time loading up his wife and son in their car, and the family set out. Travel was slow. Much of the route was unpaved and primitive. They traveled on roads that would in a few years become Route 66, the highway used by scores of "Arkies" and "Okies" traveling west in search of work during the Great Depression. The Kings drove through Arkansas and across Oklahoma, to Shamrock, Texas, a cattle town a few miles west of the Texas border.

Leaving Shamrock, they were smack dab in the heart of Texas cattle country. There were four cattle gates in the roughly one-hundred-mile stretch to Amarillo. At each stop, Beulah got out of the car to open the gate. Check then drove through and she closed the gate. Once she was settled back into the car, the Kings would continue their westward trek.

From Texas, they entered New Mexico. Arkansas is a southern temperate climate. It receives lots of rain, and the landscape is covered in unbroken green. New Mexico is arid. The brown and red rocks and the sandy soil were clearly visible through sparsely spaced piñon trees, juniper shrubs, sage, and desert brush. Even the green was a different shade. Much of the growth ranged from a deep green to olive. The mountains were rugged and rocky. And the air was dry, unlike the high humidity of the South. This was a land like nothing the small family had ever experienced.

Along the way, they picked up a hitchhiker who shared in the driving. In Flagstaff, Arizona, he wrecked the car, rendering the Kings without usable transportation. They stumbled into Phoenix low on money. Without money or transportation, Check was forced to find work, so he grabbed a job with a construction crew, building a Biltmore Hotel.

Part of the project involved building a speakeasy. Throughout the United States, speakeasies were drinkers' answer to Prohibition.[1] Typically, the entrance was built with a long maze-like hallway. At each turn, a space about the size of a coat closet was constructed on the blind side of the turn. A man with a baseball bat would then be stationed in each

---

[1] In January 1920, the Eighteenth Amendment to the Constitution of the United States went into effect. Known as the Prohibition Amendment, it made the sale and distribution of alcohol illegal.

"closet." Police knew that behind each turn, a man with a bat was waiting, ready to swing at the first law enforcement officer to turn the corner. Motivation to raid drinking establishments dwindled as the police contemplated the consequences of running through the labyrinth.

With a few paychecks under his belt, Check and his family were able to move from a tent into an apartment. Their second child, Lois Lee King, was born on August 30, 1928, in Phoenix, and the King family became four.

One morning, Check left for work with little C.T. fighting a mild cold. While at the job, Check had a premonition that something was wrong at home. He couldn't identify anything as being terribly out of sorts but going with his gut, he told his boss that he had to go home immediately. The foreman didn't want him to leave and asked Check for a reason. He said he didn't have one but believed he couldn't wait. When he arrived home, he found his son gravely ill and dying.

After C.T.'s heart-wrenching death, the Kings' great adventure lost much of its charm. The conflict with Mama Clibourn took a back seat to the need to be around family. They buried C.T., packed, and headed back to Arkansas. Riding with them was a depth of pain and grief greater than anything they had ever known.

~ ~ ~

Upon Check and Beulah's return to Conway, Arkansas, the couple tried to make peace with their great loss. Beulah showered her love onto Lois; Check swallowed his pain.

Check King had a quick temper, liked to drink, and would fight at the drop of a hat. He was also a hard worker and honest in business dealings. He was able to find work quickly, but he went from one project to another until settling into the job of selling produce to grocery stores for his brother-in-law, Dewey Wofford.

Still driven by the same entrepreneurial spirit that he had when he was producing illegal liquor, Check was determined to find another venture that would succeed. This time he confined his job search to legal opportunities.

His big break arrived when he got the chance to buy a gas station just northwest of downtown Conway at the busiest intersection in town, Highways 64 and 65. Depending on the direction one took, the roads would end at the Gulf of Mexico, the Canadian border, the Atlantic Ocean, or the Pacific Ocean. Anyone passing through town, going any direction, would drive by the 'filling station,' in the terminology of that time.

As soon as Check was in possession of the property, he went to work. The building was not much more than a thousand square feet. In the back were three rooms. Lois and her new baby sister, Betty Sue King, slept in one and the parents in the other. The third area became the family living quarters.

In the front half of the building, Check put in a café. The kitchen served both customers and the King family. In the prices of the 1940s, a hamburger on a hot bun and fried potatoes would set you back 25 cents, a steak sandwich was 15 cents, a pint of sweet milk cost 8 cents, and a large bowl of chili went for 15 cents.

Out the front door was the gas station. King's Gulf Station advertised that it was not "just the 'Fill-er-Up Kind.'" For the price of a tank of gas, the attendant would "check your battery, sweep out your floor board, check your [tire's] air [pressure] including the spare tire, and clean the wind-shield." The four pumps dispensed gas to those traveling north, south, east, or west. The location was excellent and business was good.

PLEASE ORDER BY NUMBER

Compliments of

King's Gulf Station, Roller Rink, Tourist Court and Cafe

2nd Junction U. S. Hwys 64 - 65, 1 Mile North Conway, Ark.

MENU

SANDWICHES

1. STEAK on hot-Bun .15
1-a STEAK on Bread .15
2. Hamburger, on hot-Bun .10
3. Sausage, on hot-Bun .10
3-a Sausage, on Bread .10
4. Egg, on hot-Bun .10
4-a Egg, on Bread .10
5. Fried Ham, on hot-Bun .10
5-a Boiled Ham, on Bread .10
6. Hot Cheese, on hot-Bun .10
6-a Cold Cheese, on Bread .10
7. Bacon, on hot-Bun .15
7-a Baron, on Bread .15
8. Balogna on hot-Bun .10c
8-a Balogna on Bread .10

COMBINATIONS

9. Cheese-burger, on hot-Bun .15
10. Cheese & Egg, on hot-Bun .15
10-a Cheese & Egg, on Bread .15
11. Sausage & Egg on hot-Bun .15
11-a Sausage & Egg on Bread .15
12. Ham & Egg, on hot-Bun .15
12-a Ham & Egg, on Bread .15
13. Hot Ham & Cheese, on hot-Bun .15
13-a Hot Ham & Cheese, on Bread .15
13-b Cold Ham & Cheese, on Bread .15
14. Bacon & Egg on hot-Bun .20
14-a Bacon & Egg on Bread .20

Ice Cubes per glass .05

Our Trimmings are Mustard or Sandwich Spread, Pickles, Onions and Slaw. Any or All.

Toasted Bread for Any Sandwich, 5c Extra

SOUPS & CHILI

23. Chili, large .15
24. Chili, small .10
25. Chicken Soup
26. Vegetable Soup .15
27. Vegetable Beef Soup
28. Tomato Soup .15
29. Oyster Stew .25

PLEASE ORDER BY NUMBER

The next project was the land at the top of the hill. Check built two cabins there. Beulah made the quilts and drapes, and they named it Shady Gap Tourist Court. Once the buildings were opened for business, he advertised, "Our Cabins are equipped with Butane gas, hot and cold showers, Innerspring mattresses and electricity. Being on a hill facing 64 & 65 Highway, one has an excellent view of the country and Conway, and of course, will stay cooler in summer." He catered "to tourists only." Locals were not allowed to rent, keeping the prostitutes and one-night stands away.

To the east and at the bottom of the hill, Check built a roller-skating rink. It was a screened-in wooden building with canvas tarps that could be raised for a breeze or lowered for protection from cold or rainy weather. As soon as it was completed, Lois and Betty were allowed to skate there during the day as well as in the evenings when it was open for business. Not having cold enough winters to freeze the lakes and ponds, the rink was Conway's substitute for ice skating.

By the time the King girls were in junior high school, the state's figure-skating champion lived in Conway and he enjoyed teaching the King sisters. Betty, the more athletic of the two, was especially good. Lois denied it, but it must have been a thrill for a junior high school girl to get private lessons from the Arkansas figure-skating champion.

~ ~ ~

Two of Check's younger siblings were twins: a boy named Maude and a girl named Claude. Maude liked to joke that his parents got the two confused at birth. According to Check, Maude was a Golden Glove boxer in the United States Marines, but his military career had been cut short because he was judged to be too mean. After leaving the Marines, he traveled the state burglarizing stores until he was apprehended and sent to prison.

Maude's imprisonment was a problem for all the King family. Not because they thought he was innocent; they knew he was guilty of every theft. They were disturbed though that one of their own was incarcerated – and for stealing, of all things. Maude, they felt, had tarnished the name of the entire family.

After some discussion, the family decided they were going to get Maude released, legally. Check and his uncle, Elmer Turner, canvassed the state, going to every store Maude had robbed and paying the owner back for what he had stolen. When every debt was satisfied, the family approached Arkansas Governor Carl Bailey, told him what they had done, and asked for Maude's release. When the governor hesitated, they said, "If he ever robs anyone again, we'll bring him in ourselves, and you can lock him up for good." The governor agreed, and Maude was given his freedom.

Maude left the penitentiary and went to work for Check at King's Gulf Station, Roller Rink, Tourist Court and Café. Maude hadn't been employed for long when Check noticed a large increase in oil sales. He asked Maude about it.

"Come over here." Maude took Check to a car and raised the hood.

"Now watch this." Maude pulled out the oil dipstick and wiped the oil from it. He placed the stick back in, withdrew it again, and showed it to Check. It registered one quart low.

"Okay, it needs a quart of oil," Check said.

Maude showed Check how he placed his thumb so that the dipstick did not reach fully into the oil pan, appearing to be one quart low. This maneuver was performed so skillfully that a person could watch and have no clue that he had just been swindled.

Check fired Maude on the spot.

That night, Maude knocked at the Kings' door. Check answered and stood at the screen door without inviting his brother inside.

Through the screen door, Maude said, "It ain't right, Check. I'm blood, and you don't fire your own brother. You need to be taught a lesson, and I'm here to do just that."

Check's eyes were cold and emotionless. Stepping outside, he showed no fear in facing a Golden Glove boxer.

In his deep voice and with a slow southern drawl, he said, "Maude, you can whip me, I know that. Here is how it's gonna happen. You will knock me down, and I will get right back up. Every time you knock me down, I'm gettin' back up until I'm dead. Maude, you're gonna have to kill me."

The men squared off into their fighting stances. Check the street fighter and Maude the boxing champion.

Ready to fight, the men stood waiting for one to make the first move. Unable to shake the thought that he would have to kill his own brother, Maude suddenly dropped his guard and stomped away, cursing.

It didn't take long for word to get around. Among the family it was widely believed that Maude was the better fighter — but Check was good for his word. Maude would be forced to kill him before the fight was over. Maude, saved twice by his family — the first time from prison, the second time from his own violence — changed. Soon he had a reputation within the family and larger community as a redeemed, happy, hard-working man.

~ ~ ~

King's Gulf Station was a success, but the cramped family quarters and the long hours eventually took their toll on the family. After years of operating the business, Check sold it and then purchased a business in downtown Conway. He stocked it with supplies and opened a hardware store. He also bought the family a house. No longer were they cramped into three small rooms at the back of their business.

Lois was a good student and easily material for an institution of higher learning. Fortunately, Conway wasn't like many other areas of the state and country and it was acceptable for a girl (a white girl, anyway) to attend college. There were two schools in town for her to choose from and both were within easy walking distance from the King home on Mitchell Street.

But if Lois were going to attend, she had to work. She landed a job at the J.C. Penney Company.

Penney's allowed Black and white employees to eat together. This unusual opportunity allowed Lois to engage in conversations with one Black employee. His name was Bobby, and he was about the same age as Lois. Eventually discussion turned to race relations, and Bobby told how he felt particularly dehumanized by being forced to sit at the back of the bus.

For Bobby to talk openly with Lois was risky. Under Jim Crow strictures, Black men were never to talk to white women in a familiar way. Maybe Lois won his confidence or he spoke out of the bravado of youth. It could have been as simple as a teenage crush. It is also possible that he just did not see what he had to lose. Regardless the reason for confiding in Lois, she began to question segregation. Just as was the case with her future husband, these thoughts were new and there was no one she knew discussing such radical ideas but a seed was planted.

~ ~ ~

Lois went to Arkansas State Teachers College (now the University of Central Arkansas) before transferring and graduating from Hendrix College in 1949, the first person from her immediate family and the second member of all her extended family to complete college. A cousin, Marietta Wofford, had graduated from Hendrix a few years earlier. Marietta was the daughter of the man Check worked for when he sold produce.

Check liked to say that he had gone through college twice. His joke was that he had made deliveries that required him to pass through a college campus on two separate occasions. The joke could have been his attempt to hide his regret that he never had the opportunity himself.

After Lois graduated from Hendrix, she went to work for the Women's Society of Christian Service. The WSCS was an organization of women in the Methodist Church whose mission was to assist other women in achieving their full potential. Membership was voluntary, and since the group supported equality of the races, those who joined usually shared this common value. Lois worked as a WSCS Church and Community Worker and was hired to work with youth in the town of Hope, Arkansas.

In 1948, the WSCS hosted and Lois attended a conference for Methodist women. It was held at a church camp that was established two years earlier when the Methodist Church had used a $25,000 grant to purchase Windy Willow Turkey Farm west of Little Rock. Six structures on the property were renovated, and it became Camp Aldersgate. Campers were admitted without regard to race, and the location became one of the first places in the South where interracial groups could meet.

The conference Lois attended consisted of Black and white women, and they not only discussed integration, they lived it. The entire camp — sleeping areas, restrooms, and the dining room — were fully integrated.

This was one of the first conferences of its kind in the southern United States and the first in Arkansas. Breaking the rules of segregation in 1949 was revolutionary stuff. Simply by being present, the women were making a statement that they opposed separation of the races. To cast out Jim Crow would completely overhaul the society of the South, yet these women believed it needed to be done. The discussions went far beyond the talks Lois had with Bobby.

The group believed that segregation was wrong and was in direct violation of their faith. At the end of the conference, Lois knew that segregation must end. How, neither Lois or anyone else attending knew, but the seed that was planted when Lois had discussed race with Bobby was beginning to germinate.

~ ~ ~

After only a few months of employment with the WSCS, my mother, Lois, along with two other women, was assigned to attend a training program at another Methodist camp in the Appalachian Mountains of Tennessee. One of these women she travelled with, Sally, was white, and the other woman, Mary, was Black.

It was not a simple task for an interracial group to travel together. There were rules and laws to govern their behavior throughout the entire trip. Restrooms were separated by race. The two races could not eat together in a restaurant. If they followed the proper protocol, Lois and Sally would eat in the restaurant and Mary would go to the back door, order her food, and eat outside. Mary would not be allowed to stay in the same motel as the white women anywhere on the route. When driving, the white women were required to sit together in the front or back seat while Mary always sat alone.

Sally, Mary, and Lois were all impacted by their time at Camp Aldersgate. They believed there was a different way for the races to interact, and Jim Crow, they decided, would have as little impact upon their trip as possible. For meals, Lois or Sally would go into the restaurants and order their food to go, then the three would eat in the car. For restroom breaks, they had no choice. They would stop at public parks and each would go to the facility designated for their race.

To get around the laws declaring that people of different races could only sleep in facilities designated for the individuals' own race, they decided they would not sleep; they would make the trip in one day. Finally, while in the car, they decided to alternate driving, completely ignoring the seating dictates of segregation.

~ ~ ~

Bobby, Aldersgate Camp, and Mary profoundly affected Lois. She gained a better understanding of how segregation worked its way into all aspects of a Black person's life. It was during those encounters that Jim Crow began to take on an ugly human face for her. The seed had germinated and was now growing.

The Wooden Sidewalk

Holly Grove, Arkansas, 1949–1952

The ground was still soaked from the previous night's rain as the Reverend Charles P. McDonald, Jr., the new minister at the Methodist church in Holly Grove, walked to the post office with the morning mail. Reverend Charles' first church, in 1949, was in an Arkansas Delta[2] town of a couple hundred people, and he liked to be seen making a mail run.

Being out and about early gave the impression that the new Holly Grove citizen was an industrious go-getter, but the truth was that a church of less than a hundred people left him with time on his hands. After returning from the post office, he often sat in his office and read the morning paper or slipped into the parsonage next door, where he lived alone, and grabbed a quick nap.

Slow times notwithstanding, Charles was thrilled to be in Holly Grove. He was newly ordained and serving a church. People looked to him for spiritual guidance. He was there when they celebrated births and marriages, and he gave comfort to the sick and dying. It was a wondrous calling, and he was doing exactly what he had wanted to do since he was a teenager.

---

[2] The flatlands of eastern Arkansas are commonly referred to as the "Delta." In reality, the "Delta" consists of a number of different geological regions. Holly Grove lies in the Arkansas River Valley. I will refer to the flatlands of Arkansas as the Delta. While not always technically correct, it conforms with spoken norms.

The sidewalk to the post office was wooden and elevated a few inches above the saturated ground. Stepping lightly to avoid slipping on the still damp wood, Charles followed two white men striding side by side. A lone Black man approached from the other direction. The rule, known by all, was that the Black person must step off the walkway, remove his hat, and let the white people pass. It would take a minimal effort, of course, for the two white people to move to single file and let the man pass by and stay dry. Instead, they continued walking side by side, forcing the "colored" man to step into the mud and wait for them to pass. Charles watched the entire event in silence.

This was just one more reminder to Black people of their place in society. Encounters similar to this were everyday occurrences, but this was particularly disturbing. The total disregard for the Black man's dignity sickened Charles. By the time he returned to the church office, he was livid at those who would humiliate another person and walk away seemingly without thought. The anger was also directed at his segregated community, which sanctioned this and so many other outrages. He also directed rage at himself, an ordained Methodist clergy who had witnessed something evil and remained silent.

As the twenty-two-year-old minister thought about what he had witnessed, he believed, once again, that he had to speak out. He had no idea how he would do so. This wasn't Michigan or the safe campus of SMU. There was no one he could talk to, and segregation was woven into every fabric of southern society. It was the law of the land, and terrible things happened to people who stood against it. Being white was some protection, but it did not grant total immunity.

Fear of the consequences did not change his belief that he would someday have to take a stand, but how could he protest what he had seen? He knew of no movement that would support such a dissent. The few people he knew who opposed segregation were friends from college and seminary, and they were scattered around Arkansas and the country. He could count their numbers on his fingers. The system was overwhelming; it was much bigger and more powerful than a few idealistic men in distant towns.

~ ~ ~

Holly Grove, the Delta town where Charles was serving in his first church appointment, was located approximately forty miles west of the Mississippi River, in the western region of the "Cotton Belt." Cotton, a particularly profitable and labor-intensive crop, could turn a hard-working dirt farmer into a rich plantation owner if he had a ready source of cheap labor. Slavery once filled that need. Many a southeastern farmer became wealthy off cotton and slavery in the eighteenth and nineteenth centuries; however, cotton used up the soil's nutrients and, over time, the crop became less and less profitable.

Moving to a more productive soil and away from boll weevils, farmers moved steadily west and with them, so did slavery. In the early 1800s, plantations and slavery were being established in the Lower Mississippi River Delta of Arkansas, Mississippi, and Louisiana, where the soil was particularly fertile. Regular flooding of the Mississippi River and its tributaries replenished the soil and left behind some of the world's richest farmland.

Slavery was abolished during the Civil War, but by the 1940s a system of farming called sharecropping or tenant farming was in use. Here's how it worked. White people owned almost all the land and would rent farm fields to men. Most, but not all of these tenant farmers, were Black. They were responsible for supplies, such as seeds, pesticides, and plows, which they purchased from the landowner. Since the tenant farmers rarely had the cash needed, they were "carried" or loaned the money until the crop was harvested and sold. At the end of each growing season, they settled their loans and the profit was split between the landowner and tenant farmer. It sounded good, but there was a catch, actually a couple of catches.

First, since the tenant had borrowed the operating money, he was entirely at the mercy of the landowner, who set the prices for all the supplies. Second, many, if not most, landowners 'cooked' the books, falsifying the records to show that the tenant always owed more money than he made. Once again, the tenant's debt was carried into the next year, obligating him to continue farming. Many were illiterate, but even for the individual who could read, it was of little consequence. To question a white person's honesty was strictly forbidden. Life was one of constant debt. On top of that, food, housing, and basic necessities were handed out in meager allotments. The workers caught up in this system, and their families, existed in abject poverty.

Leaving was not an option for many. They had no education or skills, and they knew little of the world outside of their farm and community. There was also the money they owed. To leave a debt without paying the balance was to default on a loan.

Some escaped in a decades-long cultural shift that became known as the Great Migration, traveling to cities in the North such as Chicago, Illinois, and St. Louis, Missouri, to settle and find work. However, fleeing the South for points north or west was not a ticket to complete freedom. No area of the country was free from prejudice, racism, and discrimination. Black people who fled the South could find themselves facing difficulties because of skin color anywhere.

Also, escapees could not return to their former homes without the possibility of capture and charged with loan defaults and/or other charges, real or imagined. White people sometimes attended funerals of Black families to look for and capture people who had fled the life of involuntary servitude. Often, the captured were given the option of returning to the life of servitude on the plantation or going to prison. Most selected the farms.

In those days, virtually all of one's daily needs — food, hardware, car supplies, clothes, and more — could be purchased in the ten or so downtown businesses that lined both sides of the railroad tracks in Holly Grove. Farming was the area's only industry, and the town's economic health was governed by how the farm fields fared. Nothing in the downtown area was much farther than a good stone's throw from farmland. Some years were better than others, but, on the whole, farming was a very prosperous business for the white landowners. If farmers had a bad year, the entire town tightened its belt. When the year was good, the town and the economy boomed.

Radical changes had taken place in Holly Grove in the previous forty years. Many of the town residents had experienced the transition from horses to the internal combustion engines that powered automobiles and tractors. Most of the more affluent homes were furnished with conveniences made possible by electricity and running water.

The Holly Grove Methodist Church was a red brick building one block northeast of downtown. It was a beautiful building, with stained-glass windows. Ceiling fans were strategically placed throughout the church to move the air around – a particularly nice touch in a region that sported long, hot, and humid summers. The church parsonage was an old white frame house adjacent to the church; its plain outside appearance hid the fact that inside, it was furnished with many modern conveniences. Like most white people's homes, it had electricity, a refrigerator, and a washing machine. It was heated with space heaters, which burned on natural gas, and the toilet was indoors.

~ ~ ~

In June 1949, only a few months before Charles watched the men on the wooden sidewalk, he drove into Holly Grove with all his worldly possessions packed into an old, dilapidated 1936 Ford. He received a salary of two hundred dollars a month and a place to live. At his father's encouragement he invested in a monthly savings bond for eighteen dollars and seventy-five cents, and he bought a one-thousand-dollar life insurance policy for thirty-two dollars a year. His only other expenses were utilities, food, and the twenty dollars a month he gave to the church.

At the end of each month, Charles was left with money in his pocket and he soon decided he needed a new car. While he was a college student, his uncle had remotely bought a car from Clarendon Ford, only a few miles outside of Holly Grove. Charles was enlisted to go to Clarendon, pick up and deliver the car to his uncle's home in northwestern Arkansas.

The car dealership owner remembered Charles and was willing to cut him a deal, so he traded his old '36 jalopy for a brand-spanking-new 1949 Ford.

The law set the maximum length of time that one could finance a car as fifteen months, so Charles landed a car payment of seventy-three dollars and sixty-three cents a month, by far his biggest budget item but easily affordable.

Charles had grown up in modest means in the Depression and had come of age in World War II. His father had lost his grocery store during the Depression, but he had been able to find work as a traveling salesman. To be able to go out and buy a new car off the lot was a new experience. He had never known the kind of money he was bringing in at Holly Grove. Charles was young and single. He had a new car and money in his pocket. Life was grand. The Reverend Charles Paul McDonald, Jr., was in high cotton.

About the only thing that was decent on his old Ford was the spare tire, and as soon as Clarendon Ford had possession of the automobile, they replaced it with one that was old and worn-out and sold the car to a Black man. It wasn't long before the new owner had a flat and realized that his spare was worthless. He promptly walked back to the dealership and requested a new one, but the salesman would not consider a replacement for a Black man.

The man must have considered his options. He could accept what the dealer told him and do nothing, or he could go to the previous owner of the car. There was little chance that he would get a new tire from a white man, but he was poor and every penny counted. Besides that, he was approaching a man of God. Maybe the Reverend would do him right. He carried the tire to Charles and asked for a replacement.

"I'm sorry but the tire was new when I traded it in. It's no longer my responsibility," Charles answered.

Jim Crow was not only a set of laws; there was an established set of rules that Black people were expected to follow. It was known as Jim Crow Etiquette. Two of those rules were:

- Never assert or even insinuate that a white person is lying.
- Never impute dishonorable intentions to a white person.

To argue would be to invite a reprimand that could range from a stern warning to physical violence. The man had no choice but to accept Charles' answer.

Two days later, the upholstery in Charles' car was slashed. Some money for a Boy Scout fund raising drive was on the front seat and it was not touched. He suspected the slasher was the owner of his former automobile who had asked for a replacement tire. Recounting this narrative fifty-five years later, Charles said, "I always felt bad about that – I should have bought the man a new tire." When Charles had said no to the request, he closed the door on any hope for fair treatment.

Don't Worry, I've Observed the Procedure in Medical School

Holly Grove, Arkansas, 1949 - 1952

Life was good. Charles McDonald was doing exactly what he wanted to do. He enjoyed and cared for the people of Holly Grove, and the people responded in kind.

One of his tasks was to work with the church youth, and in the summer of 1949, adolescents from the area churches were gathering for a weeklong conference in the nearby town of Brinkley. The teenagers from Holly Grove doubled as the work crew, and they arrived early in Brinkley to set up the chairs and tables for a meeting that was part of the conference. Hindering their progress was a group sitting in the room where they needed to do their work. Charles couldn't tell who was the leader. They all looked so young.

"Who's in charge here?" he asked.

"I am," said a beautiful black-haired, blue-eyed woman.

He was immediately smitten, but he did his duty. "I'm afraid I'm going to have to ask y'all to move. We have to get ready for our meeting."

The woman was employed by the Women's Society of Christian Service of the Methodist Church and was there with the youth from Hope. She was mildly irritated, but she kept her feelings to herself. She rounded up the teens and they went looking for another place to hang out until the conference began.

Before the week was out, Charles learned this woman's name and asked Lois Lee King for a date.

She was not on the lookout for a man. She was still a recent college graduate and was considering applying to medical school. However, women were seldom admitted into the field of medicine and she had not decided whether it was worth the trouble. Nonetheless, Charles had a pleasing personality — he liked people and people liked him. Lois said 'yes.' Their first date was while they were still in Brinkley. They went out for a Coke.

They quickly found that they had much in common. Both graduated from Hendrix College, but attended at different times. Lois' first year was only a few months after Charles' graduation. They did not know each other, but they knew many of the same people. Charles' faith was handed down to him from preceding generations. He was the most recent addition to a long line of Methodist clergy, and he had been deeply involved in the Church since he had arrived into the world. Lois, too, grew up a Methodist and was also devoted to the Church.

~ ~ ~

The two began a whirlwind romance and only a few months later, Charles asked Lois to marry him. He proposed on Skyline Drive, just outside of Conway — a favorite parking area in Lois' hometown. She accepted. On January 16, 1950, they were married at the First Methodist Church in Conway. It was the church Lois had attended all her life, and it was Charles' home church during his three years at Hendrix College.

The people of Holly Grove were excited that the church's young minister was bringing his new wife to be part of their community.

By November 2, almost ten months into their marriage, Lois was nine months pregnant and her back had hurt all day. Dorothy Richardson was a church member who was also pregnant. When she went into labor and began experiencing problems with the birth, the decision was made to take her to Memphis, two and a half hours northeast of Holly Grove. Her husband, Barner, asked Charles to drive them and he agreed. When he returned from Memphis, he told Lois he needed five good hours of sleep and she obliged. Five hours later, in the early morning hours of November 3, 1950, Lois woke her husband. He called Dr. Herb Stone, the only doctor in Holly Grove. There was no hospital, so they met Dr. Stone and his nurse at his clinic.

After he examined Lois in the delivery room, he came out to tell Charles what he had told Lois: the baby was in the breech position.

"I'd like to send Lois to Memphis like I did the Richardsons, but the baby is coming too fast so I'm going to have to deliver it here," Dr. Stone said.

He paused to give the expectant father time to process the information. Dr. Stone, like Charles, was new to his profession.

"Now, I've never delivered a breech baby before, but don't worry," he said. "I've observed the procedure in medical school and it is not at all complicated. Everything will be alright." As if to punctuate how prepared he was, Dr. Stone told Charles that he had been on a long-distance call to Memphis reviewing breech births with the Medical School there.

He turned to go back into the delivery room.

"Do you want to come in?" the doctor asked.

"Yes, I do."

True to the doctor's word, the birth went without a hitch, and Lois gave birth to their first baby boy, Charles David McDonald – the author of this book.

For thousands of years, men and women have been transformed by the birth of a child. There is something about seeing a new human being that transcends description and fills us with a sense of responsibility, and hope, and love. Seeing their first-born child did all this to my parents, and I have always known that I was loved.

~ ~ ~

The town and church congregation were ecstatic. Less than two years earlier, a single young man drove into Holly Grove in a run-down 1936 Ford. Now he had a new car, a new wife, and a brand-new baby boy.

As Thanksgiving approached, with David only a few weeks old, Lois did not know if she would be able to prepare the traditional meal. She was tired. Charles asked around and found a Black woman, Pearl, who would be willing to come in and prepare the meal. It went off perfectly. When Pearl had finished her job and it came time to pay her wages, Charles gave her almost twice the going rate. Charles knew the standard pay for a Black woman doing domestic work, and it was not a fair wage. Pearl helped out several times during the McDonalds' time in Holly Grove and, each time, Charles paid her a higher amount than she could receive anywhere else in town.

The new baby was changing the way the young couple interacted with each other. They were defining their roles in the growing family. Without being fully conscious of it, Charles and Lois entered into an unspoken contract with each other. If they were asked how the birth of a child would help them develop a strategy for confronting the issue of race, they would not have seen the two issues as related. But a time would come to speak out against the injustices of the day. Charles' voice would be heard in public. Lois would see to it that the message of equal rights was heard and understood by the children at home. This tacit contract, agreed on in Holly Grove, would serve them well.[3]

~ ~ ~

Meanwhile, the world was changing. Shortly after my birth, big news came to town. Much of the community piled into their cars and trucks to take a look at the first mechanical cotton picker in the area. Looking at the machine, Lois knew that she was watching the world as she knew it change. She didn't know what would happen, but something told her that this giant of a machine would have a major effect on the place where she lived.

"I should write this down," she thought. She never did, but she was right. This machine took the place of the large number of the laborers needed to pick cotton. At the same time Black people were denied education and training, they were finding they were no longer needed in the fields. The lives of

[3] More than two decades later, this "tacit contract" would be modified. Lois would take on work away from home and build an impressive résumé for her work with minority children and youth.

countless men and women went from bad to worse as their only work skill was being taken from them.

It appeared that no one in the church was thinking of any changes that didn't have to do with technology, especially in the area of race. In truth, most were committed to maintaining the status quo. At one church service, Charles, in his sermon, referred to a Black woman as a lady. As the congregation was leaving, one man shook Charles' hand and said, "Rev. McDonald, don't you *ever* refer to a n***** as a lady." Again, Charles remained silent.

Back home, he told Lois.

She understood. When she was still living with her parents in Conway, Check came home from a service at the Methodist church furious with the preacher for doing the same thing — referring to a Black woman as a lady.

~ ~ ~

Three months after David's birth Lois was pregnant again. Publicly and privately, the parents were thrilled. However, one thought was gnawing at the expectant couple, something they had difficulty expressing. The love they had for their one child was so intense that it didn't seem like they would have enough space left to love another infant. Would they have to take some of their feelings for David and give them to the next child, or would the next child have to survive with less love?

On December 14, 1951, Lois went into labor and just like he had done before, Dr. Stone called Charles aside and told him that this baby was breech. Dr. Stone had now been through one such birth and he was not at all nervous about the second one. This time, he did not mention the possibility of a drive to Memphis. Nor did the possibility occur to Charles. Just like the birth of David, this delivery proceeded without a problem.

They named the baby Ronald Paul McDonald. From the beginning, the parents had plenty of love for both. This gave Charles an illustration that he would use throughout his life. "Love is not like a pie," he would say. "It is not something that you cut into slices and give to each person until it runs out. The more love you give, the more you have."

For the second time in less than a year, the church members celebrated. People would drop by with food or just to say hello, but Sundays were when the church community went into action. Both McDonald boys, as well as Terry, the Richardson baby, were passed from one adult to another until every person who wanted in on the action got their chance.

Being a young mother of two children was not all fun and games. Diapers had to be washed and hung out to dry. Meals were prepared and, except for canned goods, all food was prepared from scratch. There were dishes to be washed; clothes to be cleaned, dried, and ironed; a refrigerator that required regular defrosting; and floors to be swept and mopped. The list of tasks never ended. The work of raising two boys and running a household was taking its toll on Lois, and she was exhausted.

Pearl worked for the McDonalds from time to time, but the church salary that seemed so high when the pastor was single gave a family of four barely enough money to get by. They could only afford occasional help. Charles helped around the house as much as possible, but as he came to know the people and the needs of the church, the hours he spent at work increased. He was at home less, while their growing family was sapping increasing amounts of Lois' energy.

One thing Charles could do was the shopping. He could usually break away from work and pick up any needed items. Unlike his wife, he had the luxury of being able to go into the stores without two children in tow.

~ ~ ~

There were three grocery stores in Holly Grove. One was Pat's Grocery. Pat Marshall, the owner, had a younger brother, Jack. Jack loved to fish, but he had been wounded in World War II and he couldn't get his boat in and out of the water. Charles didn't know much about fishing, but he could handle a boat. When able to get away for a couple of hours, the two would go fishing. It was a perfect combination: Charles did the heavy lifting and Jack taught Charles to fish. Jack and his brother Pat were also members of the Methodist church, so it was natural that the McDonalds would shop at Pat's Grocery.

Like the two other food stores, Pat's was small. The shelves were stocked with bread, staples, a few fresh vegetables, fruit and meat. Canned goods added variety to the regional diet. A section of the store was set aside for hardware and clothing. Fabrics were also available. The McDonald family paid cash for its purchases, but those who could not pay were "carried" or given credit. White people who needed credit were given fair terms that they could manage. For Black people, the system in the store was just like the system on the farm. The store owners calculated the interest and when the crops were in, the tenant farmers were expected to settle their debt. If they could not pay what the grocer said was due, their debt was carried over to the next year. It was just one more way that the sharecroppers and farm laborers were trapped into constant servitude.

One day while shopping, Charles strolled to the meat counter and pointed to what he wanted.

"Oh, no," Pat Marshall said. He went to the back and returned with some higher-quality meat that he wrapped and weighed.

"That meat," he said, pointing to what Charles had selected, "is for the colored people."

"That's not fair," Charles thought.

He paid for the groceries and walked home depressed and angry. This time, just like in the past, he had remained silent.

~ ~ ~

Late winter into spring was the rainy season in Arkansas. There are no hills and mountains in the Arkansas Delta and without steep terrain, water is slow to run off the land. One area can stay relatively dry while an adjoining plot of land, only a few feet lower in elevation, can flood.

The spring of 1952 had been especially wet. Lower elevations were being hit hard, but the Holly Grove Methodist Church was high and dry.

This particular Sunday morning, worship was much like any other service until an African American man slipped into the church and sat at the back. He was not noticed until a bee lit on Charles' hand and he slapped at it. The flow of the service was interrupted and the congregation was temporarily distracted. One of members' eyes landed on the Black man sitting in the back and she was noticeably shaken. Others looked and the effect was electrifying. People stared at the man with shock and horror. Charles continued with the service, but the disapproval of the people in the pews and the choir was etched on the faces and in the body language of the men and women of the church.

The worship ended as it always did, with Charles walking to the sanctuary's back door while the choir and congregation sang the benediction. The Black man was the first to leave. As he was walking out the door, Charles shook his hand, a rare occurrence between a Black man and a white man. The man quickly explained that he, too, was a Methodist pastor and that his church was flooded. He said he wanted a worship service and had decided to stop in. Then he got in his car and drove off.

Those leaving church that Sunday were not happy. One church member, Mrs. Willis, was responsible for gathering the collection plates, but she stormed home, too upset to do her job. Charles gathered in the collection and walked home, hearing a ringing phone the moment he walked in the front door. Some were convinced that this was an attempt by the man to integrate the church, while others talked openly about the need to be vigilant against this kind of behavior. Charles listened to the complaints and explained again and again that this man was a Methodist preacher and his church was flooded. No one was convinced that this was an innocent act.

Regardless of the man's intent, sitting in the back of the church that day represented a challenge to segregation and it would not go unnoticed by the church congregation. Farming was the economic lifeblood of the region and for it to be profitable, sizable tracts of land had to be farmed. That required a large work force of inexpensive labor. The mechanical picker and other technology would change the need for laborers in a few years but, in 1952, Black people provided the field hands. White people were not going to give up any of their control without a fight. In fact, no rights would be voluntarily given to Black people, including the right to worship in a white church.

Surely this man knew the risk he was taking when he decided to attend a white church. Three years later, in 1955, a woman named Rosa Parks started a bus boycott in Montgomery, Alabama, when she was too tired to relinquish her bus seat to a white person. Segregation and a hard day at work had exhausted her. Maybe this man, like Rosa Parks, was too tired to travel to a distant church where he would be accepted. Segregation might have just worn him down.

~ ~ ~

Charles' brushes with racism gave him a chance to learn. For those who opposed Jim Crow, the odds were so overwhelmingly against them that it seemed impossible to effect any change. Segregation was the law. To do battle with it was to become a criminal and subject to retaliation from the legal system, white mobs, or the Ku Klux Klan. Enforcement of the laws and customs was run exclusively by white people, who held all government offices. Black people could not vote; they owned almost no land and were denied a decent education. For both Black people and white people in the rural South, it appeared that separation of the races would last forever.

In spite of the dominance of Jim Crow, the young McDonald couple came to believe with an ever-increasing conviction that segregation was wrong. When the two white men forced the Black man to stand in the mud, Charles was not a witness to anything unusual. As in all systems that deny equal rights to a group of people, reminders to the oppressed groups were frequent. Without giving it a second thought, the two white men were sending a message to the man standing in the mud that he was the lesser person. This was probably coupled with the unspoken communication that resistance to the rules of Jim Crow by Black people or white people would be dealt with harshly. Without a shred of awareness of what they were doing, the men also helped a young Methodist pastor further cement his belief that the South's system of racial segregation was wrong.

It was also true of the man who reacted angrily to Charles referring to a Black woman as a lady. Then there was the man who asked for compensation for the tire only to be refused by Charles. The same was now true of the congregations' response to a Black minister attending their church.

But Holly Grove would never hear Charles speak out on race. In the Methodist Church, all clerical placements were evaluated each year. Those who needed or wanted to move were appointed to another church. It was a complicated process, taking months to match the right man to the right church.[4] In May of 1952, at the church's Annual Conference, it was announced that Charles was assigned to the Methodist church in the town of Ozark, Arkansas. Two of the local teens drove a borrowed farm truck loaded with the young family's possessions to Ozark.

In Holly Grove, Charles and Lois were married and started a family. They liked the people and were well liked in return. Charles was able to care for people in times of joy and of grief. Every week for three years he had, in his sermons, shared with the congregation some of his most profound beliefs. The McDonalds made friends they would know for their entire life. For all its prejudice and faults, Holly Grove was a good town.

---

[4] There were no women clergy in the Methodist Church in 1952 or at any time during this story.

When He Comes At You, He Is Going to Come Low

Ozark, Arkansas, 1952 - 1958

There are six different geographic regions of Arkansas, but to most people, it is rounded off to three: the Delta, the Hills, and the Mountains. The move from Holly Grove to Ozark was a trip of less than two hundred miles and in that distance, they left the Delta and passed into the Hills.

Over generations, the rolling landscape resulted in a population that was culturally different from that of the Delta. The Mississippi River Delta was referred by some as "the most southern area of the South." The McDonalds had found the people outgoing and the area awash in southern hospitality. By contrast, the people of Ozark were somewhat slower to reach out to the newcomers. Not that they were rude or impolite in any way. It just took them longer to warm up.

Cotton was grown in the Delta and required a large labor force. Black farmworkers had filled the need for cheap labor in the fields of Holly Grove, but Ozark did not require a large number of workhands. Unlike row crops such as cotton, cattle and poultry could often be managed by a single family. Prior to the Civil War, the hill communities had few slaves. By the end of the Civil War, slavery was gone and only three buildings in Ozark remained standing — the rest had been burned to the ground. However, neither the buildings' destruction nor the end of slavery had put the small, mostly livestock-related farms out of business.

The Black residents in the area, many of whom were presumably descendants of the region's freed slaves, lived in an area outside of town known as Adam's Mountain. Its rocky, infertile land rose above the Arkansas River and the rich river bottom soil that was in such short supply in this town.

The First Methodist Church was located two blocks west of the town square on U.S. Highway 64. It was a beautiful rock structure complete with a steeple. The cornerstone at the church says 1905, marking the beginning of the building's construction. It was five years later before the church could hold worship services in the sanctuary.

Charles' grandfather, the Reverend J.J. Galloway, had served in the Ozark church in the early 1900s, and a few of the older members remembered him. Father Galloway, as his family called him, recorded in his journal in December 1911 that he had chartered a railroad car so he could move his "cow, horse, buggy and all" to Ozark. Upon arrival, he was delighted with the town, as well as the new suit and hat that he had been given upon his arrival. "This surely is a beautiful modern church, with a pipe organ and all the modern equipment," he wrote. "May God give me success."

When Reverend Galloway had moved to Ozark, there was no electricity and the pipe organ was powered by a foot pump placed out of the congregation's sight. J.J. Galloway's son, and later Charles' uncle, Paul V. Galloway, operated the foot pump during services. During his down time, he would carve his initials, P.V.G., on the wall.[5] With the advent of electricity, the foot pump was removed, but the carvings were still clearly visible on the lower back wall of the choir loft.

---

[5] On a visit to the Ozark First United Methodist Church, I asked to be allowed to crawl back to the location of the old organ. The initials remain to this day.

The parsonage for the McDonalds was the same building that Father Galloway lived in only a decade after the turn of the century. It was built with square nails from the 1800s, and since it was not one of the buildings standing at the end of the Civil War, it was probably built sometime between 1864 and 1899. In the ensuing thirty to forty years, an indoor toilet was installed and the "two-holer" outhouse was made into a garage. (The two holes from the outhouse were still in plain view when entering the garage.) The parsonage also had gas heat, electricity, and running water. Even with these modern improvements, it was not modern. The house was slowly falling apart.

Soon after moving, Lois became pregnant for a third time. Ozark had a hospital, and the idea of giving birth at home when other options were available was unheard of. This time the baby was not breech and the birth went well. Unlike Holly Grove, Ozark had a hospital, and mothers who gave birth in its facilities stayed for ten days. When Donald Lee McDonald arrived, the building was full. The staff converted the doctor's lounge into a room for Lois. Unlike the patients' rooms, Lois' had a telephone. Ten days in the hospital with a telephone and no responsibility for cooking or cleaning gave Lois her first "vacation" in almost three years.

With three boys, baths became a challenge. The family couldn't afford to run water for each boy, so they bathed together or took turns without changing the bath water. As children do, occasionally one of the boys would release a stream of urine into the bathtub. The culprit was always, at least for that moment, the least liked member of the entire family. This went on for some time until the frustrated parents decided to ask their doctor if this was a health risk. Dr. Dwayne Brothers said there was no danger, but he was quick to point out that he did not recommend it as the preferred method of bathing.

The doctor's pronouncement that the children's health was not in jeopardy did not improve the status of the boy caught urinating in the bathtub.

The McDonalds weren't the only growing household in the Methodist parsonage, as it seemed they shared their house with another family. With three small children, sleep was already in short supply for the adults. And the other boarders, a band of packrat rodents, were loud enough to keep the parents awake at night. Every attempt to rid the house of the unwanted vermin failed. One night, in anger, Charles picked up a sledgehammer and tore out a wall trying to get to the wretched beasts. Behind the demolished wood was a nest stocked with a number of the rat family's possessions, proving the wisdom in the name "packrats." The McDonalds now had a rat-free house, but confessing his destruction of church property to the trustees was the next unpleasant task.

The next day, Charles informed the trustees that there was a large hole in the wall of the parsonage and explained how it got there. The group accepted the news with grace and agreed to have the wall replaced. Charles was given the responsibility for supervising the repairs and reporting the workmen's progress to Mr. Pitt Chancy, an older man who was already upset with the modern changes the young Reverend McDonald was implementing in the church. While Mr. Chancy was complaining about the church's departure from conventional worship, Mrs. Chancy was complaining about the number of children. "No church," she would say, "would want a preacher with such a large family. Three boys under four years old. Shameful." Little did Mrs. Chancy know that the family would soon grow while still in Ozark.

The Chancys, perturbed by Charles' lack of restraint in the destruction of that wall, kept the repair work going very slowly. Learning to deal with passive-aggressive church leaders was a skill that the young Rev. McDonald would have to learn and deal with many times in the future.

~ ~ ~

It was soon apparent that advocating for improved race relations was not as threatening in Ozark as it would have been in Holly Grove.

When Charles was attending seminary, his grandfather, J.J. Galloway, gave him a formula for espousing potentially divisive positions from the pulpit. Father Galloway said that one could say anything from the pulpit as long as it was said with love.

Charles never discussed race relations with Father Galloway, but he hoped and believed that his grandfather was someone who would support him when the time came to take a stand. Charles was missing an important point, however; the Reverend J.J. Galloway was a product of his time. In 1923 while Father Galloway was serving at the Methodist church in Morrilton, Arkansas, the Ku Klux Klan had donated $50 to the church in recognition of Galloway's good work. Nevertheless, his instruction to speak with love was one of the guiding principles Charles used when addressing race relations in Ozark and throughout his ministry.

By the time the family arrived in Ozark, Charles had become more self-confident in his role as a leader. It showed. He had been talking about race relations from the beginning of his time there, and he found an openness to his message of racial reconciliation and equality in this town of 1,700 people.

The only major complaint he received was from the director of the town's waterworks, Fred Carson. Mr. Carson adamantly opposed anyone who would treat Black people as equals. He saw Black people as less than human, and he was vocal about his beliefs. Since Charles was speaking out from the pulpit, Carson knew where Charles stood on the topic and was not at all happy. He was heard complaining about a sermon on race relations and threatening to attack Charles. Miss Elizabeth Burris, a church member, came to Charles with the threat and a helpful hint: "Charles, when he comes at you, he is going to come low."

"If he comes at me, I'm not going to find out how he fights," Charles said, laughing. "I'm gonna run."

Fortunately, Charles never had to test his running ability. Carson quit attending church and withdrew his membership.

Within a year of arriving in Ozark, Charles scheduled an integrated military choir to sing in the church. An invitation to the choir recital was sent out to the small African American community. Jim Crow dictated that Black people could only attend funerals or special events at white churches and that they were to be seated in the back of the sanctuary or in the balcony. Breaking with tradition, at this recital, Black attendees were seated throughout the sanctuary. There was little, if any, resistance to the integrated service. This was quite a difference from how the Holly Grove church reacted when the lone Black man seated himself in the back of the sanctuary. Charles' growing vision of racial equality was getting legs.

Elizabeth Burris, the women who had warned Charles of Carson's threat and brawling style, was also the outspoken editor of the town's newspaper, the *Spectator*. This was unusual, as in the 1950s, women were usually neither outspoken nor newspaper editors (with a couple of notable exceptions).

She was also a good businesswoman and understood that a good human-interest story sold newspapers.

Poochie, the McDonalds' dog, had quite a mothering instinct. U.S. 64 ran in front of the parsonage, and it was just a matter of time before Poochie crossed the highway to chase a mother cat from her litter and claimed the kittens as her own. This was important enough news for the front page of the *Spectator.* The McDonalds quickly separated Poochie from her adopted family and, in time, she became pregnant with her own puppies.

The same mothering instinct that made a cute tale then turned sour. Poochie became even more protective of her pups than she had been of the kittens. She would growl and threaten to bite anyone who tried to handle the pups. Concerned for the safety of the children, Charles and Lois were forced to give up Poochie. They found a new home for her on a farm just outside of town, and the adoptive family reported that Poochie turned into a great farm dog.

There were no pounds in Ozark, and no one the McDonalds knew bred canines for sale (only for hunting). On the remote chance that the McDonald family found a breeder, they knew the cost would be well beyond their means. So, Charles put the word out that they were looking for a replacement for Poochie.

Word traveled fast, and Charles soon heard of a litter of collies that needed a home. The McDonalds took one of the puppies, carried him home, and named him Jerry. The dog was a great pet. For one thing, when approached, he would grin — literally. The boys also had a wagon that they would sit in to be pulled by their parents. Once, when they were in the wagon, waiting for a ride, Jerry came running up, took the wooden handle in his mouth, and began pulling. He wasn't able to get up much speed or take them for a long distance, but he was an instant hit. If given a choice between having their parents trundle them long distances or having their four-legged friend take them only a few yards, at a slow pace, Jerry was the winner, hands down.

Through the years, the McDonalds always had a pet, and Jerry was the best they ever owned. But unfortunately, dogs love to hunt, and poultry is an easy and exciting target to pursue. The area around Ozark was dotted with poultry farms, and once an animal makes a kill, he or she will not stop. It supposedly "gets into the blood." Canines can also get "the scent" from eating raw poultry. Knowing that, the McDonalds were very careful about their pet's diet, never feeding him raw chicken or turkey. One night, after the kids' companion was put out for the night, he took up with a pack of dogs that were raiding turkey houses. From that point on, Jerry had the scent.

Early one morning, the pack Jerry ran with killed a man's turkeys. The farmer they raided was from Adam's Mountain, the Black section of town, but he was white. He followed Jerry to the McDonalds' house and went straight to Charles.

Being polite but firm, the man explained the situation and told Charles that he wanted to be paid for the slaughtered turkeys. Charles replied that he didn't have the cash but would pay a little each month. Feeling sympathy for the Reverend, the man said, "If you put the dog down today, we'll call it even."

One of the harsh realities of rural life was that an animal with the scent had to be eliminated. Sometimes people fenced in an entire pack of hunting dogs or chained a mean animal for the safety of the owner and visitors. Other than these few exceptions, to chain or fence in a four-legged friend was unheard of — it was never done. When an animal interfered with one's ability to earn a living, it had to go. There was no other alternative.

Crestfallen, Charles asked, "How do you suggest I do that?"

"That's up to you," the man replied, "but you have to do it today."

Charles took the short walk to see Claude Russell at his business. Between pumping gas for customers, Claude listened to Charles' predicament.

"Yes, I know a man that will do it," Claude said. "He's down by the river and he'll put down your dog for a dollar."

"How does he do that?"

"He'll shoot him."

The entire family loved Jerry, but Charles knew what was required of him. He contacted the man, who said he would meet Charles at the river.

The loved collie was loaded into the car, and Charles drove the few blocks to the Arkansas River. "Keep the dog close and try to calm him so he ain't jumpin' around," the man said. Petting and gently talking to Jerry until he relaxed, Charles stepped back. The man took aim and shot the family's most popular pet through the head. Death was instantaneous. The man picked up the carcass, careful not to put his hands on any blood, and threw it over the embankment into the water.

Fighting back tears, Charles handed the man a one-dollar bill, got into his car, and drove home.

Later that day, the children noticed Jerry was missing. The parents told them they didn't know where he was — not exactly a lie.

Rural life is not always peaceful. Communing with nature is not always soothing to the mind and soul. Charles didn't know it then, but the anguish he felt over having Jerry shot and killed would haunt him for his entire life.

~ ~ ~

Televisions were just coming onto the scene. Lois had seen one in Holly Grove a few years back when it was very much a novelty. Lois' parents, Check and Beulah King, worried that their grandchildren were growing up without the benefits of this miracle of modern science. With a television and an antenna, one could get three different stations, each broadcasting programs throughout the day. Without checking with Charles or Lois, Lois's parents, the Kings, ordered a TV and had it delivered to Ozark. As soon as it arrived and was set up, the McDonalds realized the catch. The Kings had only made the down payment, and their daughter's family was stuck with all the future payments. They reluctantly kept the television because it would have been an insult to Lois' parents to send it back, and, besides, they too were fascinated with this new piece of technology to give it up. Nevertheless, it did add a strain to an already tight budget.

There was another technology that the McDonalds found tempting regardless of the cost. It was called an air conditioner, and it would cool the air in a room enough to make a hot summer day feel like a comfortable spring day. When the temperature reached 110 degrees Fahrenheit (43 Celsius) one brutally hot summer day, the decision became easy. They bought one for the master bedroom. It was easy to install — they simply put it in the window and plugged it in. On hot days the entire family went into the bedroom to cool off.

Some historians say that a major factor in the growth of the South was the air conditioner. It took an unbearably hot summer climate and made it tolerable. The same may have been true for the McDonalds, because the family was about to grow some more.

Thomas King McDonald was the fourth boy and the third breech birth. Like the other two breeches, the delivery went without complications.

The newborn and his mother had only been home from the ten-day stay at the hospital for a short time when Lois began hemorrhaging. Charles quickly arranged for someone to watch the children and rushed her back to the hospital. While waiting for the doctor, she was given medication. Worried she might die, Lois prayed. Her main concern was what would happen to her children if she were not there. Then a thought materialized: "If I die, Charles loves our children as much as I do and he will care for them. It will be okay." She relaxed. When the doctor came into the room a few minutes later, the bleeding had stopped.

This experience became the core of Lois' faith. She believed that what happened to her was a miracle but the miracle was not that she stopped bleeding. She knew the medicine could explain that. The miracle was that when faced with a terrifying and out-of-control situation, she found the peace and serenity to stop fighting, allowing the medicine to work.

In a sense, Lois believed God tapped her on the shoulder and said, "I want you to relax and feel my presence. This is going to be okay. You are going to be okay. Whatever happens, I am with you." She was then able to let go.

This concept of God as a presence served both adults well throughout their life. They found that it worked when sick and in a hospital. It calmed them when watching a loved one face difficulties. It also strengthened their resolve when taking a stand for civil rights.

An Uneducated Plowboy

Ozark, Arkansas, 1952 - 1958

Public schools were segregated throughout the South and the justification went like this: Since Black students attended schools that were "separate but equal," there was no racial discrimination in the educational systems.

But the truth was that the systems were separate and very unequal. The school's Black students attended were always inferior. New books, for example, went to white students. When the same books were almost worn out or out-of-date, they were passed on to Black children.

It wasn't unusual for Black children to attend school in a one-room building with a dirt floor, a wood heater and an outhouse, while only a short distance away white children received their education in a modern state-of-the-art facility. In Ozark there were not enough Black students to justify a "colored school," so every morning all school-age African American students got on a bus and rode to the town of Fort Smith. In the afternoon, they got back on the bus for the return trip to Ozark. When the students stepped off the bus at Ozark, they had ridden over eighty miles and spent over two hours commuting to and from Fort Smith. Nothing, absolutely nothing was equal about segregated schools.

When Reverend McDonald spoke for integration and against the unequal treatment given to Black people, it seemed he was a voice in the wilderness. After all, what he was advocating was against the law. Segregation, especially in the schools, appeared to be a permanent fixture.

Twenty states had legally mandated segregated schools at the time. In a case challenging segregation, the United States District Court in Kansas had recently – and seemingly reluctantly – ruled in favor of segregated schools. The Kansas court ruling stated that Kansas' schools were not "separate but equal. However, the 1896 US Supreme Court decision of *Plessy v. Ferguson* upheld the separate but equal argument. The Kansas District Court could not abolish segregation in its schools as a result. Only the Supreme Court could reverse the 1896 decision.

The District Court's decision cleared the way for an appeal to the United States Supreme Court, and a team of attorneys from the National Association for the Advancement of Colored People (NAACP) promptly took action. Headed by Charles Houston and Thurgood Marshall,[6] the Supreme Court heard the NAACP appeal and after two and a half years of deliberation, the Court ruled unanimously, on May 17, 1954, that school segregation was unconstitutional and had to end. The case was popularly known as *Brown v. Board of Education*.

To call this a landmark case is an understatement. It ushered in one of the most sweeping changes the United States had ever known. For the first time, people opposed to segregation had the force of law on their side. A sleeping giant was awakening.

The McDonalds were pleased, and for a short time they naively believed that people would simply follow the law. When David enrolled for first grade in September, they thought he would be attending an integrated school. They

---

[6] Thurgood Marshall later became the first Black person appointed to the United States Supreme Court. He served from 1967 to 1991.

were wrong. Almost immediately, southern politicians and people on the streets were pledging to fight the court ruling. Charles and Lois quickly realized that integration would be a struggle. What they didn't understand was the level of difficulty that lay ahead. In the years to come, those opposed to integration would resort to extreme means to keep the races separate. Violence and murder were not uncommon. Black people were particularly vulnerable, but it was a dangerous time for anyone in the South to support racial equality.

Although there was widespread resistance to integration in the South, the strongest opposition in Arkansas came from the Delta. Cheap labor fueled the economy of the Delta, and education could threaten white people' ability to keep Black people subservient.

Of course, economics were never presented as an argument. Instead, it was alleged that Black people were intellectually and morally inferior. Since Black people could not keep up with white people, the argument went, educating the races together was unfair to both. Desegregation was setting up Black people for failure, and by slowing down the learning pace to accommodate the "inferior" students, white students would suffer by not being allowed to develop at their full potential.

Another argument against integration was that Black people and white people needed to be kept separate to protect white women. Black males, it was believed, were not capable of controlling their sex drives. To allow Black men and white women to associate would subject the women to brutal assaults and rapes. Those who put forth these arguments did so with total conviction. They did not see the most obvious contradiction: ever since slaves were brought to America, many, many white men brutally assaulted and raped Black women.

Even so-called consensual relationships between masters and slaves were assaults, as enslaved women by definition could not consent or refuse sex with their owners.

There were those in the Hills of Arkansas who held the same strong views about the inferiority of the Black race, but they didn't seem to have the tendency toward violence as those in the Delta. On August 23, only three months after the court decision, Charleston, a town across the Arkansas River and only a few miles from Ozark, admitted eleven Black students into its formerly all-white school.

In a stroke of genius, the superintendent of the Charleston schools did not publicly announce the desegregation move until September 13, three weeks after Black students were successfully integrated.[7] By that time, the community was in support of integration rendering any protester from outside Charleston unable to gain local support.

Charleston, Arkansas became the "first and only southern school in all of the eleven Confederate states to fully integrate its schools[8]." The lawyer for and on the Charleston School Board was Dale Bumpers, a Methodist and an advocate for school and church integration.[9]

After Charleston's successful and uneventful integration, the Ozark School Board and school administration did not seem to anticipate much opposition. Ozark announced its

---

7 "Desegregation of Charleston Schools," CALS Encyclopedia of Arkansas, https://encyclopediaofarkansas.net/entries/desegregation-of-charleston-schools-730/

8 Dale Bumpers, *The Best Lawyer in a One-Lawyer Town: A Memoir.* New York: Random House, 2003, 140.

9 Dale Bumpers would go on to a career as an Arkansas governor and U.S. senator.

plan to move white students and Black students into the same school in September 1957. While many southern white people were vowing to violently fight desegregation, at least in the Hills, segregation appeared to be crumbling.

At the same time Ozark was preparing to integrate, the Little Rock School District was also moving forward with a desegregation plan. When the morning arrived for nine Black students to enter classes at Little Rock's Central High School, Governor Orval Faubus posted the state militia around the school. His actions empowered those opposed to integration. The nine students showed up prepared for classes and were met by a white mob of outraged protesters. Because of a mistake in communications, one student, Elizabeth Eckford, showed up at a different spot than the other Black students and was confronted by the mob. A picture of Eckford surrounded by a mob, notebook in hand and head down, helped push Central High School into the international spotlight. The picture stunned the world and sickened the McDonalds.

The nine students who showed up at the doors of Central High School were supported by people such as Arkansan Daisy Bates, Thurgood Marshall, and on at least one occasion, Dr. Martin Luther King, Jr. President Eisenhower eventually sent in federal troops to protect them. Others helped in ways they could, but Melba Pattillo Beals detailed in her book *Warriors Don't Cry* how these nine teenagers walked into Central High School every morning to face physical and verbal abuse, with the full knowledge that there were those who would attack and, if given a chance, murder them.

In New York City a theater production was interrupted, then halted, from boos when a white actress said in her lines that she was, "a little girl from Little Rock." In Atlanta, Governor Faubus attended a Texas-Georgia football game. When it was announced that he was in the bleachers, he received a standing ovation from 33,000 supportive fans.

Internationally known trumpeter Louis Armstrong, himself a victim of segregation, canceled a goodwill tour to the communist countries of Europe, in protest of President Eisenhower's refusal to send troops into Little Rock to force integration. He told reporters that the government could "go to hell" and referred to Governor Faubus as an "uneducated plowboy." Arkansans who traveled to northern states came back with tales of people seeing their license plates and shouting obscenities at them. That same week, with little fanfare, three Black students enrolled in Ozark High School.

~ ~ ~

On the morning that the crisis at Little Rock's Central High School erupted, Charles had left early to attend the "Pastor's School" conference. It was located at Hendrix College in Conway, just thirty-five miles outside of Little Rock. Never since the Civil War had race relations become such a national crisis. Several Methodist ministers believed they were faced with a unique opportunity and, if they were to speak in one voice, their statement might be heard. They favored a petition or a public statement to express their views. As the integrationists discussed the events in Little Rock, they increasingly felt compelled to issue a press release condemning the governor's actions. They knew that they could not stop the crisis at Central High School, but they thought, as a group, they might be able to influence the course of events. They also knew they could face retaliation in their churches when they returned home. Those living in the Delta were particularly vulnerable.

Hughes was a small town in the heart of the Delta. Charles' grandfather, the Reverend J.J. Galloway, had served as pastor of the Methodist church there in the late 1920s. Now the Reverend Robert Johnson presided over the Methodist church. On the issue of race, the town of Hughes was not unlike the white congregation Charles had served in Holly Grove. Johnson begged the group of integrationists not to issue a statement. He told them he supported what the group was considering, but he could not face the consequences in Hughes if he were to sign a petition. The group understood his dilemma but also knew that a national crisis was taking place in their backyard. To delay taking action would, in effect, be a decision for inaction. They had no way of knowing how long the crisis would continue and they would not postpone the opportunity to speak in one voice.

After discussion, the group issued a statement. As reported in the *Arkansas Democrat* on September 7, 1957, the petition said, in part, that the ministers "deplored" Governor Faubus' action in posting armed troops around Central High School: "We … strongly protest the action of Gov. Orval E. Faubus in calling out the armed forces of the state to surround Central

High School ... thereby, in effect, preventing integration in compliance with the Supreme Court's decision. ... We appeal to every citizen in the state to unite with us, in earnest prayer to God that justice will be brought about, and a right example set for every child in Arkansas."

Twenty-seven church leaders signed the petition. The Reverend Robert Johnson of Hughes, like many others, was not one.

~ ~ ~

Charles and Lois had a friendly but somewhat strained relationship with Check and Beulah King. Check had a volatile temper, and, when drinking, his wrath could escalate even higher. As a child, Lois was a target of Check's sometimes violent rage. On Lois's behalf, Charles had demanded that Check not drink in the company of David, not wanting their son to experience the abuse Lois had. Check agreed, but when outside of the presence of his grandson, the game was on. He did not feel the need to restrain either his alcohol consumption or his anger.

The Kings were committed segregationists with a history of terrorizing Black people. They lived about a mile from Hendrix College, where the conference was held, and Charles felt it was only right to pay his in-laws a visit. Besides, he thought he could keep the issue of race out of the conversation. He was mistaken. The crisis at Central High School was being followed throughout the world, and the school was less than forty miles away.

From the moment Charles entered Kings' house, the discussion was about Central High. Charles told Check that he disagreed with Governor Faubus' move to stop integration. Check was aware that he was speaking to the father of his grandchildren, so he tempered his outburst. There was no threat of physical violence.

"I'll tell you why Faubus did what he did," Check declared. "We can't have colored people going to school with white boys and girls."

Charles listened for just a few minutes before he had enough.

"It's time for me to go," he said, and walked out the door. He stayed away for almost a year, and when he did return to his in-laws' house, it was only out of necessity.[10]

~ ~ ~

With the crisis raging in Little Rock, the segregationists in Ozark were emboldened. There were three Black students being sent to the once all-white Ozark High School. They were Inola West, 16; Rayford West, 18; and Nola Blanche Kuydendoll, 16. The three survived the first day without any reported injury despite an automobile driver's attempt to run

---

10 Ten years later, Check would have a stroke that forced him into semi-retirement. With time on his hands and lacking the physical strength of his earlier years, he took a serious look at his life. The anger and violence that had been a part of his early years haunted him until his death. He often talked to Charles about his fear that he would not be able to make it into heaven after the life he had led. One of the events that haunted him was when he beat a Black man unconscious for answering with a "yes" rather than a "yes, sir." He never knew how seriously he had injured the man. He sought forgiveness for this and other wrongs by donating to any Christian organization seeking money in hopes that he could buy his entry into heaven. Among his family, it is believed that he found forgiveness before his death but not because of his donations. The salvation came from the change in the way he treated others.

them down while they were walking home from school. The next day, Nola was hit with a clothes hanger and Rayford was hit in the back with a book. The Ozark school administration and board must have been under tremendous pressure, and City Marshal Dick Sowell, presumably at the direction of the school administration, ordered the students not to return to school.

One of the major state newspapers, the *Arkansas Democrat*, played down the report that someone had attempted to run over the children, referring to the incidents as "mild violence." School authorities declined to comment to the press.

Prior to integration, the move to desegregate had been labeled an "economy measure," saving the expense of busing the students all the way to Fort Smith. After the students were sent home, the school system refused to reinstate school bus transportation to Fort Smith. Riley West, the father of two of the students, was quoted as saying, "I don't know what I'm going to do now. They tell me it's too late to get the kids in school anywhere else this year. I guess I'll wait till next year and try to get them in somewhere."[11]

It appears no one thought of disciplining the perpetrators of the violence against the three high school students. Instead, Ozark's attempt to integrate the school was ended. Integration lasted only two days.

~ ~ ~

At the beginning of that week in September when Charles McDonald had left Ozark for the Pastor's School conference, the town was enrolling the three Black students in high

---

[11] *Arkansas Democrat*, September 12, 1957.

school, Central High School was planning to admit Black students, and the name "Little Rock" was seldom heard by people outside of the South. When he returned at the end of the week, Ozark had halted voluntary integration and warned its Black students to stay home. Central High School in Little Rock was surrounded by troops. Little Rock had become known throughout the world. Twenty-seven Methodist ministers at the conference had gone on record protesting the actions of the governor of Arkansas. No one in Ozark mentioned the petition.

Returning from the Pastor's School conference gave Charles a different outlook. He saw that like-minded people needed to speak as one voice during such a crisis. Although the ministers' contribution was small and had not changed the outcome, they had been heard.

Another development stemming from the Central High crisis was the expansion of the role of race relations at Camp Aldersgate, a Methodist facility outside of Little Rock. It was there that Lois had her first and only experience, at that point, of living in a fully integrated community. The camp had stuck to the belief in equality. With the Central High crisis, the retreat became one of the few places that the "leaders, parents and students of both races could meet to try to resolve the situations. Threats and harassing phone calls were made to many of those involved, and the State Police monitored who entered the camp by taking license plate numbers."[12] But the site stayed true to its beliefs and continued to take an active role in racial reconciliation.

---

[12] *Camp Aldersgate, A Brief History* (Little Rock, Arkansas: Camp Aldersgate, Inc.: 1997), 18.

Soon after the Central High crisis, the Reverend Arthur Terry, a close friend of Charles' grandfather, J.J. Galloway, sent word that he was coming through town and would stop for a visit. Rev. Terry had lived with Father Galloway and his family while he attended college.

When the Galloways, Charles' mother's family, migrated to Arkansas from South Carolina, they left behind a past as slave owners. There also is no mention in Charles' grandfather's journal of any distaste of slavery or Jim Crow. And, as stated earlier, J.J. Galloway took pride in support he received from the KKK. If Charles had paid attention to his own family ancestry, the McDonald couple probably would not have hoped for support from his grandfather's close friend but naively, they thought support of their views on race was forthcoming.

Much to their disappointment, Reverend Terry began spewing prejudice and bigotry as soon as he arrived. Rev. Terry's outburst revealed to the young couple that support would not be coming from either Charles' or Lois' families. When it came to race, the McDonalds would have to go it alone.

~ ~ ~

In June of 1958, after six years in Ozark, Charles was appointed to the First Methodist Church in Pocahontas, Arkansas. The McDonalds had arrived in Ozark believing that the customs and laws regarding race relations were wrong. As they prepared to leave, the customs were the same. With very few exceptions, all of Arkansas was still segregated. But many of the laws were breaking down, and those that had not changed were under attack. Lois not only supported her husband's ministry but shared his growing conviction in racial equality. Regardless of the personal struggles they would face, they were a team.

Catch a Tater by His Toe

Pocahontas, Arkansas, 1958 - 1961

Pocahontas is in Arkansas' hill country, but just barely. The eastern section of town bordered the Black River, and that is where the Delta and the Hills collide. With a population of 3,800, Pocahontas was larger than Holly Grove and Ozark combined.

Just as it had been in Holly Grove and Ozark, the McDonalds arrived with little knowledge of the community. Driving into Pocahontas with all their possessions was the entire family's first view of the community. One of the first things the family noticed was the brick parsonage. The days of living in an old house falling apart at the seams were over. The building was a modern home with a window air conditioner in the master bedroom. A gas furnace was recessed into the floor in the hallway and covered with a heavy steel grate. A great deal of heat came through the floor, enough to heat the entire residence. They knew they would have to watch the kids come winter. To step or crawl on the metal would cause a serious burn.

The next-door neighbor, Mr. Dreyer, owned a beautiful two-story house. He had come to Pocahontas from Germany to study cotton production when World War II broke out and was forced to wait out the war in America. During that time, he took up the hobby of horticulture. At the end of the war, he discovered that all of his considerable wealth in Germany was gone. His country was in shambles, and there was nothing to go back to. The war refugee then converted his hobby into a vocation. He became a gardener, and nowhere was his green thumb more evident than in his own house and the surrounding yard. In June, when the McDonalds arrived at their new home, their neighbor's yard was covered in flowers of all kinds and colors. Except in the dead of winter, his yard was always in full bloom.

They also had a clothes dryer they brought with them but, like in Ozark, they seldom used it, mainly because it cost a lot to operate. The machine also required constant attention. The temperature could not be regulated, so if it was left running for too long the clothes could be scorched and ruined. Still, it was nice to have when the weather turned rainy for several days and they couldn't hang the clothes out to dry. In Ozark, they had glassed in their back porch to add a bedroom for the growing family, but in Pocahontas, the parsonage had three bedrooms. And in preparation for the McDonalds' young children, a fence was put up in the backyard. The house was solid, and, for the first time, the McDonalds didn't feel a cold breeze blowing through the living room on windy winter days.

Inside and out, the house was a child- and family-friendly environment, with one exception: the floor furnace. No one gave it much thought until the first winter when someone dropped a cloth on the furnace grate and it caught fire. No harm was done, but it frightened the parents. "What if there was a fire and the boys couldn't get out?" they asked each other.

The solution was to have fire drills. The entire family began to practice getting out of the house through the windows. It was deadly serious for the adults but just another game for the children.

~ ~ ~

While in Pocahontas, the McDonald family had their fifth baby, James Daniel McDonald. The brothers were, from oldest to youngest, David, Ron, Don, Tom, and, now, Jim.

With five boys, Charles took to bragging that he now had a basketball team, and there were times when it seemed that a tournament was being played in and around the Methodist parsonage. Boys were running everywhere. If they couldn't go outside, they played their games inside. Anything could become a prop for the numerous activities the boys were engaged in. A discarded box became a fort, the hill in the backyard could be a strategic point in one of the great battles of World War II, and a cinderblock might be the perfect home plate in a sandlot baseball game. Through the years, cinderblocks, bricks, and rocks for bases frequently inflicted cuts and bruises.

When not involved in the games of their own creation, David and Ron also played in organized baseball, were active in Boy Scouts, and, of course, went to school. Tom and Jim were in diapers and making messes with toys. Don, the middle child, whom Lois and Charles called "Tag-Along," was generally following the older boys or leading the younger ones in play. It was a very busy household.

The residence was also crowded. Room sizes were small, and with five boys sharing two bedrooms, there was barely enough room for the beds. It seemed like there was always someone waiting for his turn in the bathroom. One of the boys took up reading *Mad* magazine, a popular monthly for preadolescent boys, in the bathroom. When the boys were not waiting for their turn, it became a source of humor (read ridicule). However, it was not so funny when they were waiting in line. Evidently this brother was more interested in reading *Mad* magazine than in being on good terms with his siblings.

Bathrooms became a far greater issue when the McDonalds went for a visit with Lois' sister, Betty King Welch. Uncle Tom and Aunt Betty had three children: two girls and one boy; so, eight males and four females were sharing their one bathroom. Betty grew increasingly frustrated at the boys missing the toilet so she hung a sign on the wall for the boys to see as they relieved themselves. This sign went up with every visit and came down as soon as the McDonald boys were gone. It read, *We Aim to Please, You Aim Too, Please.*

A far more important issue, race, was often discussed at the McDonald home. The boys were taught that prejudice was wrong, period. Many sayings and expressions of the day used racist terms, and the older boys heard them at school. In the

McDonald house, the use of any bigoted language was strictly forbidden. It ranked equal to the "don't you dare say that word" list and was as prohibited as the worse profanity. When the boys came home from school or play with an unacceptable saying, Lois would, if necessary, create an alternative ditty. One rhyme she changed was, "Eennie, meanie, minie, moe, catch a n***** by his toes. If he hollers make him pay..." When the boys brought the words home, she told them that was not correct. Not knowing what to replace the offending words with, she improvised, "Eennie, meanie, minie, moe, catch a tater by his toe. If he hollers make him pay..." While not a catchy phrase or one that made sense, it was the best she could come up with on such short notice, and all the McDonald boys grew up with that rhyme.

~ ~ ~

From the beginning of his time in Pocahontas, Charles preached what he called the "gospel of inclusion." He often talked about race relations in his sermons because he believed that Christianity was not a segregated faith, and that the way to demonstrate one's convictions was by treating others with respect and compassion.

The Christian Bible contains "the Parable of the Good Samaritan." It is an account of a man who is beaten, robbed, and left for dead. Several important people walk by and rather than stop and help the man, they move to the other side of the road and pass by, offering no assistance. Finally, a Samaritan, a man of low status, walks up and stops to help the injured man. The Good Samaritan was one of Charles' favorite passages from the Bible. To him it demonstrated the way Christians should behave toward others, regardless of their color, class, or religion.

A few members of the congregation had similar thoughts. One was Adrian White, the owner of KPOC, the local radio station. For years KPOC had broadcast the Sunday morning Methodist Church service.

Among the others were Jim McDaniel, a World War II combat veteran and owner of McDaniel's Hardware Store, and Gardener McNutt, who ran McNutt Funeral Home with his brother. Before long, Adrian, Jim, Gardener, and Charles were a core group who met for coffee and camaraderie. Race was a frequent topic of conversation.

At this time, Governor Faubus had already made a name for himself as an avid segregationist and was continuing his effort to keep the educational system segregated. In 1958, he closed the high schools in Little Rock rather than allow desegregation to continue. But the federal government was putting increasing pressure on institutes throughout Arkansas to merge and desegregate. In response, Faubus was threatening to shut down schools across the state.

When the governor closed the high schools in Little Rock, his approval ratings soared, and the McDonalds were worried that he might succeed in ending public education in Arkansas. They were not going to stay in Arkansas if there were no schools, so Reverend McDonald began making inquiries about moving to other states.

He contacted his uncle, the Reverend Paul Galloway at Boston Avenue Methodist Church in Tulsa, Oklahoma. It was one of the largest, if not the largest, Methodist church in the country and Uncle Paul carried considerable influence. When Galloway got the news that Charles was looking to move, he secured an appointment for him in Oklahoma.

It would be a big promotion, but Charles did not like the political manner in which the appointment was made. He declined. Galloway did not understand why his nephew would turn down such a nice promotion and tried to convince him to take the opportunity. Charles stood his ground and remained in Pocahontas. While he was grateful for Galloway's help, he didn't want to be promoted because of his family connection. Believing his decision was correct, he felt no regrets about continuing in Pocahontas.

Shortly after declining the job in Oklahoma, he was offered a job as chaplain at the Methodist Hospital in Memphis. Charles' uncle also had his hand in this opportunity. Inquiring into the hospital's practices, he learned that staff did not treat Black patients equally to white patients. In regards to race relations, a move to Memphis would be going from the pot into the frying pan, and over Galloway's strong objections, Charles turned down this second opportunity. In time, Faubus' threats to close the schools beyond the 1958–59 year never materialized so the job search died a natural death. The McDonalds settled into the town of Pocahontas and the state of Arkansas.

~ ~ ~

It was a pleasant spring morning in May, and Charles was the first to rise. He dressed and went straight to the kitchen, where he threw bacon on the skillet and started the morning coffee to percolating. The smell spread throughout the house and one by one the boys hopped out of bed and followed their noses to their father. Saturday was usually a slow day for the McDonalds. When the table was set and the food ready, Charles said a blessing and the boys ate quickly. They finished, rushed to the den, and glued themselves to the Saturday morning cartoons on television.

After the boys were settled, Lois crawled out of bed, poured a cup of coffee, and sat at the table. Charles joined her. In a few minutes, he planned to walk the short distance to the church. There, he would put the finishing touches on his Sunday sermon and take care of any church business that was not completed during the week. He was usually home by noon.

The telephone rang and Charles went into the hall. He answered and spoke briefly to the caller.

"That was Mrs. Eddie Mae McDonald," he told Lois. "She's a Negro woman and she asked me to come to her house. She wants to tell me about something that happened to her this week."

"That's all she said, that she wants to tell you about something?"

"That's it. I have no clue what she wants." Charles smiled. "I must admit, I'm curious."

Never had Reverend McDonald received a call from an African American woman asking to speak to him at her home. In truth, he had never received a call from any Black man or woman asking him to come to their house. In 1959 there was no need to discuss the significance of the call. Both knew this was not an ordinary pastoral visit.

"How do you know her?"

"I don't know her. She said we've never met."

"What are you going to do?" Lois asked.

"I told her I would be there in a few minutes."

"Let me know what happens."

"I will," he said, walking out the door.

In the few minutes it took to reach Mrs. McDonald's house he passed from the comfortable, spacious homes of the white residents to the smaller, inadequately constructed buildings of Pocahontas' poorer Negro citizens.

Arriving at the house on Smithville Street, he stopped and looked around. He noticed chicken coops and gardens where green lawns would be in his neighborhood, and he knew the reason why. For the poor, a yard was a resource that needed to be used. They could not afford to waste the land around their homes producing grass.

In May, the spring rains combined with the warming temperatures had a dramatic effect on the gardens. The plants were exploding with growth, and a few of the early vegetables were beginning to yield their bounty.

The house was a small, wood-framed building. It sat back about twenty-five to thirty feet from the dirt road that ran in front of it.

A slight chill still hung in the air from the night before. Charles got out of the car and walked to the front door. He knocked.

The door opened and the Reverend saw a woman around fifty years old and he judged her to be about 5'6" tall. She had a gentle demeanor, but there was a look on her face that was not easy to interpret. It could have been sadness, nervousness, or both.

"Reverend McDonald, please come in."

"Thank you, Mrs. McDonald."

"Most people call me Miss Eddie Mae," she said. "When I moved to Pocahontas, I was Eddie Mae Herron. I married a pastor, a Reverend McDonald — same name as you. But the name Miss Eddie Mae stuck."

Seated in the living room, Miss Eddie Mae offered tea or coffee. As was the custom, they began with some polite small talk, but when the serious conversation began, it was awkward and brief.

Miss Eddie Mae came to the point. "Reverend McDonald, have you ever heard about 'Colored Day' in Memphis?"

"No, ma'am, I haven't," Charles answered. His response was one of respect. White people did not generally address Black people by ma'am or sir.

"One day each week, Negroes can take their children to the zoo. We can't go any other day," Miss Eddie Mae said and then paused.

"I'm a teacher at the Pocahontas Colored School, and I took my students on a field trip to the zoo this week. When we got to Memphis, we decided to eat before going to the zoo, so we went to Overton Park. We were just getting ready when a police car came at us with sirens blaring and lights flashing. Two policemen jumped out of their car shouting all kinds of vulgarities and racial slurs. One of the officers was swinging his club in the air like he wanted to beat us. They said we were in the white area of the park. They acted like we were some kind of filthy animals. If I had argued or said anything that they didn't like, it's no telling what the police would have done. All I could do was to tell them how sorry I was.

"We were scared and got on the bus as fast as we could, then we drove to the zoo. When we got there, they told us that we were there on the wrong day. One man kept pointing to a sign that said Colored Day was on Thursday, acting like we were ignorant and couldn't read.

"We drove through Memphis and stopped for a parade. Even the parades were segregated. One section was for Negroes and one for white people."

For a moment Charles thought she was going to cry, but she gathered in her emotions and looked directly at him. "My students watched me apologize to the policemen while they were abusive and calling my children and me such terrible names.

"There was nothing I could do. I teach my students to respect the law and that policemen are there to help them. How can I teach them to respect the law when the police threaten us, curse us, and call us foul, racist names? What do I tell them now?"

It was clear to Charles that he and Miss Eddie Mae lived in different worlds. This was the first time he had ever spoken with a Black person about segregation, and he was listening to a woman tell a story about a situation that his wife, his children, and he would never experience.

The room was silent. People seek counsel with clergy hoping to hear something that would help them through their problems. The only comfort Reverend McDonald could give was, "I'm sorry for what happened to you, and I'm very sorry for what happened to your students. It was wrong."

"I had to tell somebody, Reverend McDonald. Thank you for coming to see me. You are a good man."

Leaving his first ministerial visit to an African American, he was unable to offer any words of comfort. There was nothing he could say to her that would change the reality.

Shaken by what had happened, he wanted to share with his wife what he had just experienced. Rather than go to the church as he planned, Charles drove home. Lois took one look at him when he walked in the door. "What's wrong?"

The everyday reality for Black people in the South was, for that moment, also a reality for Charles. He sat at the table and with tears in his eyes, said to Lois, "Have you ever heard of Colored Day at the Memphis Zoo?"

~ ~ ~

Maybe Miss Eddie Mae had heard a sermon by Charles on the local radio station, KPOC. Maybe she had heard talk about the white men who were meeting in public and discussing integration. Whatever the reason, she believed there was a white man who didn't think like the others and she wanted to tell him about her collision with Jim Crow.

For Miss Eddie Mae to talk to the pastor took courage. If Charles had reacted poorly to her, the consequences could have been grave. All Charles would need to do was tell members of the white community of their conversation and Miss Eddie Mae would have faced retaliation. Most likely she would have lost her job and been unable to find any employment in or around Pocahontas. To get any kind of work, she would then be forced to move far away from the town where she had had the conversation with the white minister. Or it could have been worse. While Pocahontas was not as violent as areas of the Deep South, lynching was not unknown.

After their first visit, Miss Eddie Mae and Charles became friends. They talked and visited several times. They joked about having the same last name and the possibility that they were related. Even teasing about being related had an ominous side. Arkansas still had the "one-drop" law, which stated that if a person had "one drop" of Negro blood they must live as a colored person, with all the rules and restrictions of being relegated to that race.

The Pocahontas Colored School went through the eighth grade before the children were sent to a segregated high school in Newport, fifty-two miles away. When Miss Eddie

Mae asked Charles to speak at a commencement service for her graduates, he was honored. The exact words he spoke to the students have been lost, but Charles remembers telling them that they were children of God and they should be proud of who they were.

Ron attended the service with his father. After the service, Ron asked why the people shouted when his father was talking. It is a reply known as "call and response." His father simply told him that was the way they worship.

Charles never forgot Miss Eddie Mae.[13] Once again, he made the same pledge that he had made many times before that he would do something about the injustice. This time it felt different. There was an active and growing movement for civil rights, and there were now laws against segregation. Often those laws were ignored, but maybe the time to stand up and be counted had arrived.

~ ~ ~

In 1945, while attending a conference in Michigan, he had roomed with an African American man. Later, while he was in seminary in Texas, he roomed with fellow students who questioned the segregation of the day. A few years later, he witnessed a Black man being forced to stand in the mud in Holly Grove, Arkansas. Now, on a late spring day, he had his first face-to-face conversation with a Black person who described segregation in very personal terms. For the remainder

---

[13] The Pocahontas Colored School is now a museum and community center. It is named the Herron Center after Miss Eddie Mae Herron, her name before her marriage. http://www.herroncenter.org/

of his days, Charles would credit these four events with changing the direction of his life.

I'm As Near As Your Telephone

Despite the Montgomery Bus Boycotts, *Brown v. the Board of Education,* and the integration of Central High School, the Civil Rights Movement had lost some of its momentum by 1960. In February, that changed when four African American college students sat at a segregated lunch counter in the Woolworth's Department Store in Greensboro, North Carolina, and refused to get up until they were served.

Their actions became known as a sit-in. This type of protest played a big part in reviving the Civil Rights Movement, and sit-ins sprang up in other cities. Jim Crow was slowly collapsing, but there remained organizations and people determined to maintain the status quo.

~ ~ ~

On March 29 of that year, Charles received a call from his friend Adrian White at the radio station KPOC. "Charles, I have something that I want to show you," Adrian said. "You need to come over and see this."

"I'll be right over," Charles answered.

Adrian was waiting when Charles walked into the radio station. "Read this," he said, handing Charles a four-page document. "I think you will find it interesting."

It was a press release from Charles and Lois' alma mater and spiritual home, Hendrix College. Fifteen years earlier, while a student at Hendrix, Charles had met Julius Scott and questioned segregation for the first time. It had been at

Hendrix three years earlier that Charles and twenty-six others had released a statement opposing Governor Faubus' order to bar Black students from Central High School. Reading the text, he felt betrayed and sickened.

The press release read:

> The Hendrix College Board of Trustees voted today to continue the College's long-standing policy of accepting white students only.
>
> Trustees in a formal statement said they are convinced that the majority of Methodists in Arkansas want the College's admission policy to remain as it now is. Hendrix is owned and operated by the Arkansas Methodist Church.
>
> Action followed a year's study of the matter by the Board's executive committee, says the statement, including many individual conferences with church leaders throughout the state, both ministers and laymen.
>
> Today's decision does not mean that the Methodist Church is ignoring the educational needs of Negroes, Bishop Paul E. Martin of Little Rock, presiding bishop of this area, said following the trustees' action. Methodists also operate Philander Smith College, Negro Institution at Little Rock, he pointed out.
>
> "For almost a century," said the bishop, "the Methodist Church had been actively engaged in a program of Christian education for the Negro youth of Arkansas. Arkansas Methodists are proud of Philander Smith, which holds the same accreditation that Hendrix does for the North Central Association of Schools and Colleges."

> President Marshall T. Steel of Hendrix said that he was in accord with the action of the trustees.
>
> "The College and its trustees have had this very complex question under close consideration for several years," he said. "Trustees are aware of their great responsibility. Hendrix is an agency of the Methodist Church in Arkansas; the trustees have tried to act in accordance with their appraisal of the wishes of the Church."

When Charles finished reading, he turned to Adrian. "This is a Christian college; I can't believe this. They should be accepting Negroes, not turning them away."

"What are you going to do?"

"I don't know. Can you make me a copy?"

"I'll do it now."

Adrian went to the printer and ran off another copy of the press release. That afternoon, Charles went home and showed Lois the article. It was no surprise that she shared his disgust with their alma mater.

"I'm going to call Bill Wilder," Charles said.

~ ~ ~

The Reverend Bill Wilder was another Arkansan serving in the town of Van Buren. Wilder was three years older than Charles, and they had grown up in the same town, Fort Smith. His mother died when he was very young, and his father raised him and his two brothers. His father sold New York Life Insurance and was uninvolved in his children's lives, leaving Wilder and his brothers to pretty much fend for themselves. Wilder graduated from high school and completed a couple of years at West Arkansas Community College before transferring to Hendrix. After graduating from Hendrix, he attended seminary at SMU. The two young seminarians always ran in different circles, and they had not yet developed the close friendship that was soon to come and would last a lifetime.

In 1958, Van Buren, Arkansas, was battling over the school district's plan to desegregate the town's high school. When the Reverend Bill Wilder publicly voiced his support for integration, a large group of white citizens and students were protesting the school's plan to integrate the classrooms. On September 9, the chief of police added his support to the white protesters by comparing them to participants in the Boston Tea Party. This inflamed the anger and added more fuel to an already dangerous situation. Wilder's response was to become more outspoken. He harshly criticized any resemblance between those protesting integration and the Boston Tea Partiers.

On the same day, the school board was scheduled for a regular monthly meeting. Approximately one hundred people showed up in protest of the school's plan to integrate.

Also attending the board meeting was Angie Evans, the fifteen-year-old president of the student council and a member of Wilder's church. She requested to speak, and the board allowed it. Evans told of a poll that she and some of her friends took of the Van Buren high school students, which showed that the vast majority of students either supported integration or didn't care if Black people were to attend the all-white schools. She then addressed the school board saying, "We think it is only fair that the Negroes be permitted to attend the high school." She also went on to complain that the protesters at the school were disorderly, used abusive language, and painted and distributed abusive posters.

Angry protesters interrupted Evans, charging that the school board had coached her. She denied the allegation, saying, "I just don't think segregation is a Christian thing."

Wilder and Evans' willingness to speak up defused a very dangerous confrontation. Over the next two weeks, the resistance weakened and the Van Buran Public Schools integrated without violence. Wilder and Evans drew national attention.

It was a testament to their growing friendship that Charles thought of calling Bill Wilder after he read the Hendrix press release on that spring day in 1960. Both men were graduates of Hendrix, and Charles certainly knew where Wilder stood on the issue of integration. Probably every Methodist clergy in Arkansas knew where Wilder stood.

Upon reading the press release, Wilder was as outraged as Charles – possibly more. The men agreed that they would individually draft and mail letters of protest to many of the board members of Hendrix and to the college president. Charles wrote:

> March 31, 1960
>
> Dear Mr. Steel:
>
> ...As a Methodist Minister and as an alumnus of Hendrix I want to voice my protest. For a good while I have felt that Hendrix should open her doors to all qualified students because I cannot understand a Christian college refusing to admit any young person solely on the basis of race.

> Perhaps the church people as a whole are in favor of segregation, but to me, the principals of Christ should supersede the thoughts of people. If our Church is to proclaim the gospel of Christ it cannot compromise and preach what the people want to hear. Our Methodist Church has made it very clear that it is opposed to segregation because it is contrary to the teachings of Christ. This action of our Methodist College is contrary to the stand of The Methodist Church.
>
> I am sure I do not realize all the problems involved but my sincere opinion is that this action is not based on the principles of Christianity.
>
> I sincerely hope and pray that the Board of Trustees will reconsider this action.

Charles mailed his letter to twelve board members.

That same day, Bill Wilder mailed an even more provocative letter to Dr. Marshall Steel, the president of Hendrix.

> March 31, 1960
>
> Dear Dr. Steel:
>
> I was sickened as I read in the Gazette of the decision of the Hendrix Trustees concerning segregation, and your concurrence in that decision. Perhaps the most unfortunate part of this decision is that it places our church in the untenable position of accepting the desires of people, rather than holding up the standards of Christian brotherhood and The Methodist Discipline.
>
> ...

> As a minister in The Methodist Church, I feel betrayed by your action. The effectiveness of what I, or any other local pastor, may have to say on Christian brotherhood as it applies to race relations is pretty well destroyed by leadership in high places which blandly assumes we must go along with the crowd!
>
> I recognize that this move on the part of the trustees will be considered "Good economics!" But I wish to express my own conviction that it was a poor move, and that ultimately it will cause more harm than good.
>
> I have always admired you, and still do. But I still hope to see you utilizing your great influence to lead Hendrix to opening its doors to all qualified students, regardless of race or creed.

Wilder forwarded a copy to his boss, Paul E. Martin, the bishop of the Arkansas/Louisiana area. Another copy went to Dr. Paul Bumpers, one of the twenty-seven signers of the 1957 petition supporting integration. Still another copy was sent to Charles. It is likely he mailed it to others as well. Wilder did not shy away from a fight.

Upon receiving and reading Wilder's letter, Charles thought of the time Wilder was a strong member of the high school debate team. He had clearly not lost that skill. "It is good to have Bill on my side," he thought, grinning.

Unlike Charles, Bishop Martin did not appreciate Wilder's letter. The bishop took no disciplinary action against Wilder, but he interpreted the words as a personal attack on Hendrix President Marshall Steel, the Board of Trustees, and himself.

Reactions from the board members regarding McDonald's letter were mixed. Many responded immediately. Some of the letters survive today and offer a look into the thoughts of a few of the more powerful people in the state of Arkansas in 1960.

G.C. Hardin was a wealthy lawyer in Charles' hometown and an acquaintance of his mother and father. He wrote:

> Dear Charles:
>
> Your letter of yesterday is acknowledged. I am quite willing to accord sincerity to your attitude, which is shared by a good many young people, in regard to this integration deal. But I want you to understand that I do not agree with you at all. I think it is quite un-Christian for the White Race to integrate with the Negro Race. Christ never taught any such thing. It is an attitude which is unrealistic and fanciful. It grieves me to see fine young people like you embrace such doctrines. I know the Negro. I know him thoroughly and feel that I have a reasonably good conscience and understanding of Christianity and sincerely hope that such movement as is current among the young people might soon be changed. Those of us who have lived long enough and have had experience know we cannot turn things over to those who have had no experience. If we did that we would be very derelict in our duty, and as for me and my part, it won't be done.
>
> Kindest regards.
>
> Sincerely your friend,
>
> G.C. Hardin

Another friend of Charles' parents wrote.

> Dear Charles:
>
> I appreciate very much your letter of March 31, which I have read very carefully and given considerable thought to its contents. …
>
> Much can be said on both sides, but, unfortunately, we degenerated into a situation in which it is difficult to have a reasonable discussion between white people, or between Negroes, or between the two races. I have some good friends among the Negroes in Clarksville who say they do not want integration and my conclusion is that they want many other considerations much more. My own opinion is that integration should not be the goal, but there are areas in which there should be some integration. In other words, everything should be done to help the Negro develop his full potential. That not only is a moral proposition, but for the good of the country this must be done, … because we have so little common labor any more. …
>
> Thank you for writing me.
>
> With kindest regards and best wishes to you and your good family.
>
> Sincerely yours,
>
> Leslie

To have a friend of his parents write in opposition to Charles' letter stung, but it was not unexpected. Experience had taught him to not depend on support from family or close friends when the subject was civil rights or race relations.

The two hoped to gain some support from other clergy that sat on the board. Both men had known Reverend Fred Roebuck all their lives. He served the First Methodist Church in Fort Smith, their hometown. Roebuck wrote:

> My dear Charles:
>
> I received your note this morning, and I am not surprised at your attitude in the matter of integration for Hendrix College, for I, too, have feelings in that same direction and wish our whole problem of integration were already solved, but it seems to be far from it. … Dr. Steel said the mail man brought him many, many letters protesting integration and threatening to withdraw their children or not to let them enter next September if integration should be brought about. … Of course, when it comes to right, it seems to some that the college should be integrated at any cost, but it seems right to others to build the college up to a strong point and be better prepared for integration when it will come eventually. I repeat that I have mixed feelings in the matter and wish I knew how to settle the problem of integration in church and school.
>
> Trusting that you are having a good year in your work at Pocahontas, and with kindest personal regards, I am
>
> Sincerely,
>
> Fred G. Roebuck

This letter was disappointing. He was a fellow clergy and knew Charles' grandfather and parents. Although strong opposition to integration would not come from Roebuck, support, too, would not be forthcoming. This may have been the most disturbing response. Many opposed integration out of a conviction that it was wrong. Dr. Roebuck had the conviction that segregation was wrong, but he did not speak his belief publicly because he was worried about the money that Hendrix would lose. In the language of his faith, Fred Roebuck would sell his soul for thirty pieces of silver.

Another clergyman's lack of support was expected but also disappointing. Bishop Paul Martin was the bishop for the Arkansas/Louisiana area, and he was Bill Wilder and Charles' boss.

> Dear Charles:
>
> I am glad you wrote to me and sent me a copy of your letter to Doctor Steel. As you said in your letter to Doctor Steel, many problems are involved in the way in which we face the matters concerning race.
>
> I do know that the Board of Trustees of Hendrix College gave a year to the study of this matter and that the Board is composed of sincere men who are trying earnestly to follow the Will of Christ.
>
> With kindest regards, I am
>
> Sincerely yours,
>
> E. Martin

Hendrix's president Dr. Marshall Steel, wrote, "I am sorry that you feel as you do about the situation. … I hope you and other friends of the College will give the Trustees credit for trying to do what, in their judgment, seems to be the best thing for the College in the light of all of its responsibilities."

There was one board member who argued against Hendrix's decision. The Reverend A.W. Martin worked as the director of the Wesley Foundation, a Methodist student center at the University of Arkansas. The University of Arkansas had already integrated by 1960. Martin was a loud, outspoken man who was not at all intimidated by authority. Protocol dictated that Methodists address bishops by their title. Martin, however, seemed to be oblivious to that expectation and would irritate Charles' uncle, Paul Galloway, by always addressing him as Paul — even after Galloway became a bishop.

In spite of being much older than most integrationists, Martin felt as strongly about the issue as Charles and his peers. He had been one of the signers of the petition protesting Governor Faubus' action at Central High.

He sent Charles a two-page letter harshly criticizing the board for its decision. A few excerpts from the letter follow:

> It is unbelievable that otherwise good men should be so blind and prejudiced in one particular area of their thinking.
>
> Interestingly enough, no one so much as suggested that what they were doing was right. The sole argument advanced in support of the Board action was that "this is what the majority of Methodist people in Arkansas want."
>
> In this background there seems to be a paralyzing fear that grips the minds and hearts of Methodist leaders in Arkansas. …
>
> It has been quite some time since I have heard any expression of concern on the part of responsible leaders in the Methodist Church in Arkansas for the role that a

> church related college should play in clarifying and practicing the principles and procedures that presumably might lead our people out of this wilderness of fear and prejudice. March 29th will, in my opinion, be remembered as a dark day in the life of Hendrix and of Arkansas Methodism. The far-reaching implications of the Board's action are staggering.

Soon after the board announced its whites-only policy, *The College Profile*, the Hendrix student newspaper, came out in support of the trustees' decision. Hendrix College seemed content to stay in the status quo.

In spite of the opposition to integration from the board, the influence of people with money and power, and the Hendrix student body's support of the status quo, there remained a small band of Methodists who were not about to let the issue die. They found it particularly disturbing that their denomination would sanction what they saw as a flagrant violation of the principles and teachings of their Church and faith. Throughout April and May, their conversations strengthened their conviction that Hendrix College could not continue on its present course. Other private and public colleges and universities in Arkansas were integrating, and if Hendrix was going to live up to its Christian responsibilities, it had to do the same.

June was Annual Conference time for Methodists in Arkansas. The 1960 conference was held at the top of Mount Sequoyah, a Methodist retreat center in the Ozark Mountains overlooking Fayetteville. In the early 1900s, Charles' grandparents, William Edgar McDonald and Nora Ellen Compton McDonald, had settled there after arriving from Texas in a covered wagon. There were breathtaking views of the surrounding Ozarks, but it was a harsh, unproductive land. The soil was rocky and infertile, and water quickly ran off the land, leaving the area high and dry. After Charles' grandfather failed in agriculture on Mount Sequoyah and built a sorghum mill in Lincoln, Arkansas, the Methodist Church bought a large tract of land on the mountain and built a retreat.

The Annual Conference was where church assignments for clergy were made official and business on a state level was transacted. The budget for the state administrative office was presented and voted on by the representative of the individual churches and clergy. The Church also ratified funding for various missions. One of the missions that the Church funded was for Jon Guthrie, an agriculture missionary to the Congo. As a youth, Jon first came to know Lois when she worked for the Women's Society of Christian Service in 1949. Jon was particularly disturbed that he could not bring his Black friends from the Congo to Arkansas, and he particularly found it offensive that he could not even take these friends to a meal at Hendrix College.

Conference was also the time that attendees got together to discuss what had transpired the previous year, and Hendrix's 1960 whites-only policy was a topic of discussion. Three ministers – Jim Beal, Bill Wilder, and Charles McDonald – requested a meeting room and invited a group of like-minded clergy to meet with them. No administrator was present, nor was the bishop asked to attend. The three fellows knew that most, if not all, of the administration would oppose any pro-integration action taken by the group, and that the bishop had publicly supported the Hendrix board's decision to bar Black students from campus.

When all the invited were present, they quickly agreed that they would present a resolution to the entire gathering calling for Hendrix College to integrate. The men readied a resolution and were prepared to present it on the conference floor.[14]

They believed this would force the hand of every member of the conference. Those opposing integration would have to publicly declare their views, which went against the principles advocated by the national body of the Methodist Church. Since the highly publicized Central High crisis took place less than three years earlier, Arkansas' steps forward or backward on integration were followed throughout the country. The resolution and the debate that ensued could conceivably receive national attention, putting further pressure on people to vote in support of the resolution.

Many in the room believed it only fair to first meet with the college president, Dr. Marshall Steel, before presenting the resolution to the conference. Steel was invited, and he elected to join the men.

Upon hearing the resolution, Steel suggested they would be more successful if they took their concerns directly to the Hendrix Board of Trustees. Steel spoke to their idealism, and he argued that members of the board were reasonable men and would listen to their concerns. The men in the room, most of whom were Hendrix graduates, had a deep love for the Church. They wanted the Methodist Church and Hendrix College to change, but they did not want to damage the two institutions by staging a public fight over integration. They agreed with Steel and appointed the three original members

---

[14] James T. Clemons and Kelly L. Farr, eds., *Crisis of Conscience: Arkansas Methodists and the Civil Rights Struggle* (Little Rock: Butler Center for Arkansas Studies, 2007), 71.

of their group — Jim Beal, Bill Wilder, and Charles McDonald — to prepare and present a petition to the Hendrix board. Steel agreed to allow the three men to speak at the next board meeting.

President Steel may or may not have personally opposed integration, but he certainly did not think the time was right. In contrast, the group of ministers favored integration and were not content to wait for some future date. However, in the first round of this conflict, Steel had a significant advantage. The clergy were young, idealistic, and naïve, and Steel better understood the politics of the time and Hendrix's board. He outmaneuvered the young men on three counts. First, after the crisis at Central High in Little Rock, national attention was on the state of Arkansas. By keeping the resolution off the conference floor and out of the media, he would not have to deal with any bad press. Second, Steel reduced the number of people protesting the policy down to a mere three. And, finally, he was able to postpone a conversation on the issue until the next board meeting, three months in the future. Momentum would be lost, and those in the room would be scattered throughout the state, losing the ability to act as one body.

~ ~ ~

The Annual Conference ended, and everyone returned home. Those who were assigned to new churches and towns prepared for their move. Charles was assigned again to Pocahontas, and the McDonalds were pleased. It was nice to stay in a place where others shared their views on race relations. The children were happy in school, and Pocahontas was a good match for the McDonalds.

Dr. Marshall Steel sent a letter thanking Charles for "the chance to visit with you and other ministers who were interested in the policies of Hendrix College." [15] McDonald, Wilder, and Beal began work on what they would present to the Hendrix Board of Trustees. After the men were in agreement with what should be in the petition, Charles put it down on pen and paper. All approved of the finished text, and they waited for word from Steel that they were on the agenda to address the board. As the time for each of board meetings approached, they were told that they would have to wait. Steel said that he had not been able to schedule the three men because of more pressing business.

At last, in April of 1961, after a full ten months' wait, Steel informed the men that they were scheduled to address the board. April was the last board meeting before the Annual Conference in June. Steel may have scheduled the men then because he realized that if they were not put on the agenda in April, they would report to the next Annual Conference that they had not been allowed to address the board.

The petition was dusted off, and Charles made copies for the board on the church mimeograph machine.

~ ~ ~

---

[15] Clemons and Farr, *Crisis of Conscience*, 76. In an oral history interview in 1979, Steel said, "[T]hey didn't represent the [Methodist] church. They represented themselves, and maybe they represented people that I didn't know about. I'm sure that I did not like the idea of their coming to the board and going over my head with recommendations to it. I'm sure I told them not to do it that way. … I felt these young fellows were adding to my problem. I was working on the matter. I wasn't working as fast as they wanted it."

In April in Arkansas, leaves suddenly appear on the deciduous trees. Seemingly overnight, the state bursts into the brilliant greens of spring. The wheat that was planted in the fall grows tall, and the fields turn first green, then gold. Farmers plow the land, and the fresh smell of turned soil fills the air. As other young crops take root, fields changed from brown to green. Dogwoods and azaleas bloom in their brilliant colors, and the world comes to life.

Each man passed through different areas on their drive to Hendrix, but they all drove through a countryside that was springing to life. The relaxed pace of winter had given way to the hurried pace of the growing seasons, with farmers working in the fields. However, these men were too nervous to take much notice. Their minds were on what they would say to the board members when they tried to persuade them to change a policy that had been in effect since the day of the college founding in 1884.

When the three arrived, they were seated outside the boardroom. They understood the reality in front of them and knew they were swimming upstream. A large majority of the board opposed integration, and the likelihood of a change in policy was remote at best. They also knew that the civility they were shown when they arrived masked the fact that many on the board deeply resented their position.

Just as he had at the Annual Conference, Steel argued that the board was made up of honorable and upright members who would work with the group without involving outside forces, such as the media. There would be no bad press when the decision to exclude Black people from Hendrix was upheld.

It was also not lost upon the petitioners that there was a new board member. Kenneth Pope had become the bishop, replacing Paul Martin. Holding the top position in the Methodist Church in Arkansas, Pope carried a great deal of influence, but he was new and no one knew where the new bishop stood on the topic of integration.

The meeting began, and Jim Beal presented the board with a petition signed by the three ministers:

> The Board's report last Spring indicated that the admission policy action was taken because it was felt that this expressed the wishes of the majority of the Methodists in Arkansas. This may or may not be, and yet, many of us hoped to see the Board take a position of responsible leadership in this important area of human relations, even as the College has led in other areas. Many things seem in the Board's favor in such courageous action: There is the uncompromising Christian ethic which implies that love for God means love for man, all men. ...[16]
>
> Our African and Asian brothers are looking to us as the witnesses of Jesus Christ, and too often we disappoint them. The witness of such missionaries as Jon Guthrie, a graduate of Hendrix now serving in Elizabethville, Republic of Congo, is hampered by this action of the Board. Of course, it isn't just this action, it's the whole image of America in this area of Brotherhood. These things would seem to say that the matter before us is one we must keep open for discussion.

---

[16] In the conventional language of the day, this reference to "men" meant "men and women."

Citing precedence, the petition then identified a number of Arkansas colleges and universities that had already integrated. Beal continued:

> The New Testament teaches us that Christ came to break down the middle wall of the partition which divides people. We hope that we can all feel that this is part of <u>our</u> mission in the world. …
>
> We are not necessarily asking you to take specific action today. Rather, we would like for you to consider some possibilities for action.

The petition went on to propose several ways Hendrix students could begin having increased contact with people of color, including an exchange program with Philander Smith College, the predominately Black Methodist college in Little Rock.

After they read the petition, the men were thanked and dismissed.

The agreement to not talk to the media gave Steel and the board a tremendous advantage. The board could act or not act, with impunity. Few of the board members bothered to respond. Bishop Pope sent a letter of support for the "three Fellows" that met with the Hendrix board, and Marshall Steel sent a letter thanking Charles for attending the meeting. They also received at least one letter of support from board member and Little Rock lawyer Graham Hall:

> As to Hendrix, I believe that the first step should be the smallest possible one. That is the acceptance of one negro female student who would have room and board

> in Conway rather than on the campus. I have had the records searched at the negro high school here and I have had personal interviews. This inquiry has brought to light a negro female student whose I.Q. test appears to be higher than any white student in the Little Rock Public School System.

(Mr. Hall was probably referring to one of the two students that would integrate Hendrix three years later.)

Less than a month after the meeting with the board, a group of white and Black activists known as the Freedom Riders left Washington D.C., intent on challenging segregation in the South. Breaking with the rules of segregation, white people sat in the back of the bus and Black people took the front seats. At each stop the white people used the "colored" facilities and the Black people used the restrooms designated for white people.

It was a treacherous ride. Their buses were stoned and bombed. Riders were beaten and jailed. They never made it to their destination of New Orleans because the riders were arrested and jailed in Jackson, Mississippi, but their journey drew the entire nation's attention to their cause.

Central High School has desegregated after an ugly fight, many Arkansas colleges and universities were admitting Black students, and the Freedom Riders had faced violence traveling through the South, but Hendrix College stayed the course. It remained a committed whites-only school.

Back in Pocahontas, life went on without any visible change. Charles continued to preach, and the McDonald family continued to enjoy the town.

~ ~ ~

However, it was not business-as-usual for all Arkansas Methodists. Bishop Kenneth Pope stated publicly that segregation was wrong, and he was making moves to confront the issue. He had been favorably impressed when McDonald, Wilder, and Beal stood in front of the Hendrix board. What he said to the board behind closed doors is not known, but following the board meeting, he told Charles' uncle, Paul Galloway, that he intended to appoint Charles to the position of District Superintendent, a church administrative position.

Just a month after the board was petitioned by the three men, on a Wednesday in May, Charles received a call from the bishop. Pope had rethought his idea that Charles should be a District Superintendent. The bishop had another plan. He wanted Charles to move to the Little Rock Conference, which covered the southern half of Arkansas.

The McDonalds were in the North Arkansas Conference, and church policy required the minister's consent to change conferences. Charles would have to agree to a move to southern Arkansas.

The move would take the McDonalds to the "Deep South" area of the state, where most white people were strong segregationists. A move to southern Arkansas would undoubtedly put Charles' beliefs in direct conflict with the overwhelming majority of his parishioners.

He believed to the depths of his soul the words that he wrote in the petition to the Hendrix board. "There [is] an uncompromising Christian ethic which implies that love for God means love for man, all men." To remain silent was not an option. He also knew that there were a few in the Little Rock Conference speaking out. When they did, they always faced strong opposition from their congregation. Charles asked Pope for some time to think on this request.

~ ~ ~

The first step in this decision was to tell Lois what he had been asked to do. She too understood the problems her family could confront with the move, but she also shared her husband's view on the issue of race. She was willing to move south.

In the church parsonage, the living room was always off limits except for holding church-related functions or hosting visitors. In a house with five boys, it was necessary to have a clean room when people came to visit; the only way to keep the room up to standards was to make it out-of-bounds.

Charles settled into the only place in the house where he had any hope of solitude while he debated his options while Lois attempted to keep the boys from trying to get in to ask their father what he was doing.

The decision was a simple one. The family could relocate to a church in southern Arkansas or Charles could turn down the request and remain in the North Arkansas Conference. From time to time, Lois joined her husband in the living room while he struggled with the decision.

He thought of the resistance that he, Beal, and Wilder had encountered when they went in front of the Hendrix board. When Wilder took a public stand for integration of the schools in Van Buren, the hostility he faced was staggering. Although there was no violence, Wilder was fortunate to have made it through that crisis without experiencing physical attacks.

Try as he might, Charles couldn't shake the memory of entering the ministry twelve years earlier and making a personal vow that he would never turn down a church appointment. It wasn't a promise he made lightly. He believed it to be part of a sacred covenant he had with God. He also vowed that he would speak truth in the face of injustice and would respond to hate with love. The ministry Charles believed he was called to was not a ministry of convenience. When confronted with prejudice, his sacred vow required him to take a stand.

For several hours he sat, unable to sort out the conflicting thoughts. Could he subject himself and his family to the certainty that there would be trouble when he relocated south?

Eventually, Charles' attention was drawn to a picture of Jesus that hung on the wall. As he stared at the picture, he contemplated his covenant with God to serve wherever called. To refuse to move was to turn his back on his sacred duty, and that he could not do. He would tell the bishop his fears, but if the request remained for the McDonalds to move conferences, they would go.

Before he made his decision final, he spoke with Lois. Lois was not only his wife, but she was his partner in all things. She shared his belief in racial equality, but she, probably more than Charles, understood that the safety of the five children she was raising could be at risk.

Lois agreed to the family moving. She never spoke of the decision as being difficult, but she must have known that to agree to the move potentially put her, her husband, and her children at risk.

Three hours after walking into the living room, Charles went into the hall and picked up the phone. When Bishop Pope answered, Charles spoke of the problems he knew he would face. Pope thanked Charles and said he would soon know the town where the McDonalds would move.

True to his word, Bishop Pope called the next morning.

"Charles, I would like you to go to DeWitt."

DeWitt was a town of three thousand people and in the heart of the Mississippi River Delta.

For the second time, Charles put all his concerns on the table.

Pope listened respectfully, then said, "Don't worry, Charles, I'm as near as your telephone."

How is that going to help when I'm facing an angry congregation? he thought. But he kept the words to himself.

Instead, the Reverend Charles P. McDonald, Jr., told the bishop, "I have never refused a move. You can send me to DeWitt."

He hung up the phone and told Lois. In less than one month, the family would be living in this new town.

They were going back to where their life together had begun, the Arkansas Delta.

A Fierce Fighter Which Was Best Left Alone

DeWitt, 1961 - 1965

Within minutes of the family arriving in DeWitt, church members were dropping by to meet the McDonalds. Entire families were visiting, and every one of the McDonald boys was welcomed with open arms. Before their first day was out, the older boys were signed up for summer baseball, the family had learned the location of the city pool, and the kids had made a multitude of new friends. David and Ron had already visited some of their new friends' homes.

Adults presented food dishes to hold the McDonalds over until they settled in. New farming machinery and modern methods had made rice the most profitable crop for the Delta, and the preacher and his wife marveled at the number of dishes that were prepared with this grain. The town was awash in southern hospitality, and by the end of the day all the family was excited and looking forward to life in this new town.

The McDonalds were putting down roots in an area known as the Grand Prairie. It had the same rich Delta soil as Holly Grove, and, like in Holly Grove, farming was the lifeblood of the community.

Outside of agriculture, there were only two major employers: a shoe factory and the school system. Those two "industries" employed only a small fraction of the population, however. Many of those working in the schools were wives providing a supplement to their husbands' farm income.

Sports, hunting, fishing, and church provided the major diversions from work.

Standing water attracted mosquitoes and water moccasin snakes in copious numbers. Water was everywhere — in rice fields, bayous, marshes, and swampy terrain. Mosquitoes came out in the evening and stayed active until morning. That night, when the family was safely inside, Charles entertained them with stories about these bugs. It wasn't just people who needed protection, animals had to be sheltered at night, too. This pest is the deadliest animal on earth, and Charles brought home tales about horses being found near death from these blood suckers after being left outside for only a couple of nights. The McDonalds were to learn that the mosquito stories were true and the insects were every bit as bad as their reputation. In the summer, all outdoor activities had to take place in the daylight hours. Little League baseball games were played only in the heat of the day. There were no evening games.

Water moccasins were also known as cottonmouths for the solid white mouths they showed in preparation to strike. All four species of venomous snakes — rattlesnakes, coral snakes, copperheads, and cottonmouths — found in North America resided in the rural areas of Arkansas. The cottonmouth was the most aggressive and very dangerous. When threatened, it tried to flee, but if no escape was immediately evident, it would coil and bare its venomous fangs. The sight of the white, open mouth was a reminder that one was facing a fierce fighter which was best left alone.

In Pocahontas, the boys were allowed to traverse through the woods and creeks looking for adventure. They also had a swimming hole that they would go to from time to time. In DeWitt, the boys were strictly forbidden from placing a foot in the water. If not for the snakes, the irrigation ditches would have served as a great place to take a dip on a hot day.

Luckily, there was the city pool. It was inexpensive, had lifeguards, and was open to any white child in town. Ron and David spent that summer playing baseball, swimming, and getting to know other kids around town.

The most popular activities in town were sports and hunting. The town loved high school football and basketball. In summer, there were both sandlot and organized baseball. Hunting was mostly a men's sport and took place in the winter when they were free of their farming responsibilities. People hunted all the game animals associated with the South. There were deer, rabbits, quails, and squirrels, and since a duck migratory route called the Mississippi Flyway passed over DeWitt, duck season was the major hunting highlight of the year.

~ ~ ~

Except for Holly Grove, no place the McDonalds had lived had stronger enforcement of the laws of segregation than DeWitt. Social contact between the races was strictly forbidden. Probably the most serious offense was a romantic encounter between a white woman and a Black man. It was of little concern that the same kind of encounter between a Black woman and a white man was tolerated as long as it was out of sight. It didn't matter that these sexual relations were often rapes. As long as it was hidden, it was accepted. The evidence was all over town. Black people were all shades, from almost white to coal-black, testifying to the liaisons that had taken place between the races going back to the days of slavery.

Water fountains, bathrooms, and waiting rooms were segregated. DeWitt was the county seat, and the segregated facilities of the county office building in the center of the town square were especially noticeable. Signs were posted above water fountains and restrooms as "Colored" or "White." White people considered Black people dirty, and they commonly thought that using the colored facilities would expose them to a host of dangerous germs.

For a Black man or woman to use a white facility was illegal. All restaurants in the white section of town were off limits to Black people. Should a Black person want to buy a meal at one of those establishments, he or she would go to the back door, out of sight of the white customers, place an order, and wait outside for the food to be brought out.

The theater on the town square was segregated, and Black moviegoers were restricted to the balcony. Stores would not wait on a Black person until all white customers were served. The Black section of town was referred to as "the hill" or "n***** hill." Black people could live only on the hill.

Then there was the Ku Klux Klan, the terrorist group that enforced the laws and customs of segregation. In 1961, the Klan's influence was on the decline, but it was still very much alive and influential in the South. A cross burning was a recognized symbol of the KKK and one of its most powerful tactics. It is hard to imagine the terror that a family must have experienced when they looked out of their window and saw a cross burning in the front yard. It was a warning to anyone, Black or white, that retaliation for disobeying any of the rules and laws of segregation could involve violence, torture, and death. Tragically, there was no one to turn to for protection; the legal system simply looked the other way.

None of the McDonalds ever saw a cross burning, but the terrorist message was understood by all southerners, Black and white. The use of the cross was especially galling to

Charles and Lois. To have the symbol of their faith used to symbolize hate and violence was a hideous distortion of all they believed. At one time, the Klan was active in DeWitt, but the McDonalds never knew if the Klan had died out or just gone underground.

It may seem amazing that separation of the races was so accepted in a town of only 3,019 people, but the rules were so embedded in society that everyone played out their day-to-day roles without notice. Segregation was like a finely oiled machine, all the moving parts operating in perfect sync. For white people, segregation appeared to operate easily and by mutual consent. In reality, however, the separation of the races took place by force. Tune-ups to the Jim Crow machine were brutal and happened mostly out of the sight of the greater white population. There were areas of the South where public violence was practiced, but DeWitt was not one of those towns.

Part Two

~

Taking a Public Stand

We Reserve the Right to Refuse Service to Anyone

DeWitt, 1961 - 1965

I am the oldest of the five McDonald boys who rode into DeWitt in late spring of 1961. I was ten years old, had just finished the fifth grade, and was obsessed with baseball. Other than being forbidden to use the racist language I heard all around me, I was not aware that there was anything different about my family. I have no memory of talking or hearing about segregation prior to moving to DeWitt. It was in this Delta town that I first began to understand the racism of my community.

Talk of race was everywhere. I only remember two kinds of racial conversations: there was talk about the inferiority of Black people and there were racial slurs. Among the many racial slurs, the word "n*****" was arguably the most common.

It was used in the name of foods, in common phrases, and in slang terms. Children's ditties included phrases such as "catch a n***** by his toe" and "last one home's a n***** baby." Brazil nuts were sold under the name "n***** toes"—a name also used to refer to a common confectionary. And there was an entire genre of "n***** jokes" that depicted Black people as lazy, shiftless, and ignorant.

As a teenager I began hearing what might have been the most racist of the many phrases. When referring to a dark-skinned white person or an ignorant person, it was said that there was "a n***** in the woodpile." When I asked my mother what it meant, I was told that this referred to the custom of a white man fathering children from a Black woman.

No doubt, many of these sexual encounters were rapes and/or extreme abuses of power that white men inflicted on Black women with impunity. That white men raped and brutalized African Americans again and again without any regard for their humanity is one of the harshest legacies of my race.

All in all, I doubt that a day passed that I did not hear Black people referred to by white people in a racist manner. Already knowing that I was not supposed to use these words and phrases, I took what I heard to Mother and she explained the meaning to me. She did not condemn the people who said these things, but she left me with no doubt that to use racist language was wrong.

From the beginning, I believed my parents' strongly held beliefs were right because they were my mother and father. In this community, I was soon to learn to understand segregation on my own.

~ ~ ~

My first memory of segregation was when I was eleven years old. My mother sent me to pick up some items from the hardware store at the town square, four blocks away from our house. I liked going there because it was run by the Schallhorn family. Johnny and his wife, Lou Cree, were a young couple who attended my father's church. Johnny worked at Schallhorn Hardware, and Lou Cree worked as my dad's secretary at the church. They were fun to be around, and on the few occasions that my parents went out without us, they babysat. They were the only adults I was allowed to address by their first names, and they always had a friendly greeting and a quick and easy laugh.

The retail section was a large room about the size of a convenience store with shelves and displays throughout. The store was stocked with hardware supplies such as nuts, bolts, and hand tools, and a myriad of other products lined the shelves and floor space. Items were not prepackaged and were placed on the shelves or stored in the back. Nails of all sizes were stored in rotating bins. It looked something like a giant steel lazy susan, and the clerk turned the bin around until he got to the requested nails. He then raked the nails into a paper bag with a garden hand rake and weighed the bag and its contents on the nearby scale. Nails were sold by weight, and it amazed me how any one of the clerks could come within a few nails of the weight requested.

Since we were a farming community, the hardware store also stocked small agriculture supplies like hand plows, garden seeds, and fertilizer. Major farm implements were sold at the farm supply store.

The room carried the slight smell of the items throughout: oil from the protective coat placed on tools, the earthiness of the garden seeds, the sweet and sour scent of fertilizer, and, of course, the aroma of coffee. All these scents combined to give the place a barely detectable rough, masculine odor.

The doors were open and ceiling fans were cranked up to the highest setting, but the air movement provided little relief from the heat and humidity.

A clerk helped me with my purchase and when I had my order, he moved on to someone else while I walked toward the line of people waiting to pay.

As soon as I reached the back of the line, everyone stepped aside to allow me to go first. I was confused and became more so when the clerk told me that I should step forward and pay. "But these people were ahead of me," I replied.

The clerk looked directly at me and calmly replied, "They'll wait, you can go first." I walked to the front of the line and paid my bill. On the walk back to our house, I marveled at how nice the adults were to let me go ahead of them.

At home, I told Mother how I was allowed to go to the front of the line. I had her total attention when she asked, "Were the people standing in line Negroes?" The question surprised me. I didn't immediately know the answer, but after a moment of thought, I told her they were.

With a look of disgust and in an angry voice, Mother said, "Because you are white and they are Negroes, they had to let you go first. It's wrong." That was the first time I remember seeing the finely oiled Jim Crow machine in action; segregation had left the dinner table discussions and entered into my life.

To have this conversation with my mother in a white southern home in 1961 was an amazing event. My brothers and I were the only ones I knew who lived in a home where no one was allowed to use the word "n*****." I was taught that it was a terrible word.

The phrase "n*****-lover" was another frequently heard term that we weren't allowed to use. It was considered a major insult, but, in my family, we were told that if that term was directed at us, we should be proud. Mother told us that to be called a "n*****-lover" meant that we were treating all people as human beings. If we could do that, we were being good Christians and good people.

My mother was going far beyond simply teaching her sons that the use of racial slurs was wrong. She was telling us that the way of life in the South was wrong. Our economic and social systems were rooted in segregation, and it was widely believed by white people that without segregation and Jim Crow our whole way of life would crumble.

In those days, the *only* place I heard that segregation was wrong was in my home. There may have been other parents telling their children the same thing, but I never heard of it. As unlikely as it may seem, I never discussed race with any of my friends, but I feel certain that very few parents told their children what my mother told me on that day.

~ ~ ~

During our first year in DeWitt, when I was in the sixth grade, I got a paper route delivering the *Arkansas Gazette*. My job was to substitute for the regular paperboy on days he couldn't throw the newspapers. On those mornings, I would get up before school to pick up, roll, and deliver the news on my bicycle. The papers were delivered to me outside a diner where people came for breakfast and camaraderie before going off to the fields or to their businesses for the day. When the weather was bad or when it was very cold, Dad drove me around town on my route.

One morning when he was helping me, we sat outside and got ready for the route. Preparing the newspaper was a craft that I prided myself in doing skillfully and fast. It involved rolling the newspaper and tying it with string that uncoiled from a large spool. If it was raining, I would wrap the newspaper in waxed paper.

Dad and I went into the restaurant for a quick breakfast before getting started. We sat at the counter, and I pointed to a sign that was prominently displayed on the wall of the diner. It read, *"We reserve the right to refuse service to anyone."* I thought it was there so the owners could tell troublemakers to leave, but when I asked Dad about it, he said that that was not the reason. He said that the sign was there to warn Negroes that they would not be served in the restaurant.

He spoke quietly but forcefully, and the intensity of his response gave me the clear impression that the sign represented something very bad. I can still recall the disapproval on my father's face and in his words. I always liked going to that restaurant in the morning. It was where the early birds went, and I had felt I was part of a special fraternity. From that day on, the restaurant lost much of its appeal.

~ ~ ~

Maybe it was because of the hardware store and the diner. Or it could have been that I was hearing of the evils of segregation at home. It is also possible I was just getting old enough to understand. For one or all of these reasons, I was becoming more aware of what was happening around me.

One of my most powerful memories of segregation happened right across the street, in our neighbor's yard.

Money was not in great supply in our family, but I was given an allowance of seventy-five cents each week. I was required to save twenty-five cents and to give twenty-five cents to the church. That left me with a mere quarter for my own use. If I wanted to get anything other than an occasional soft drink or to go to a movie from time to time, I had to come up with other sources of income. My brother Ron and I picked up some spending money mowing lawns and helping friends with odd jobs from time to time, but we were usually on the lookout for additional ways to make extra money.

I noticed and was paying attention to a large collection of soft drink bottles in our neighbor's backyard. In DeWitt there was no garbage pickup. Every house had a fifty-five-gallon drum that was kept in the backyard to burn trash. Our neighbor, Mrs. Mildred Robins, had her servant throw the bottles in her backyard next to the garbage barrel.

Thinking it would not be a problem, I decided to ask permission from the employee of Mrs. Robins to collect the bottles, take them to the store, and cash them in for the deposits. The bottles could be redeemed for two cents each and with my finely honed math skills, I easily calculated that a dozen bottles would mean I'd be only one cent short of doubling my disposable income for the week.

Our neighbor was a wealthy and bigoted woman. She proudly displayed in her front yard a whipping post that had been used on slaves, and she would not allow pennies in her house because of the picture of Abraham Lincoln on the coin. An exception was made for a five-dollar bill and a luxury Lincoln Town Car.

She referred to her servant only as "Monkey" or "my house nigger." No other name would suffice, and she showed no consideration whether her servant was present or not.

One day I saw him working in the backyard near the trash barrel. I ran over to him and asked if I could take the bottles that were thrown out with the trash. A look of panic came across his face. He quickly looked down and turned so he was not facing me directly. Huge pecan trees shaded the backyard, and he seemed to almost disappear into the shadows. "Oh no, if I were to give you those bottles, I would lose my job."

Even as a child, I understood what had just transpired. This man whose name I did not even know was terrified of what could happen to him if he were to give me, without permission, a few discarded soft drink bottles. Mrs. Robins had control of this man's destiny, and she had that control for one reason: the color of his skin. The man's terror was contagious, and I became frightened. I didn't want to make matters worse, and the only thing I could think to do was to leave, never to return to Mrs. Robins' house.

Today, remembering this event is painful. This was the first time I recall seeing the horror of racism without needing to have my parents interpret. Mrs. Robins' servant was not only being mistreated, he was being robbed of his dignity and humanity. I was a witness and I understood.[17]

While I was planning my entrepreneurial scheme, I didn't know Mrs. Robins had recently had a falling out with my mother. Mrs. Robins had dropped in for a visit while Mother was cleaning our fish tank. Our neighbor brought up the riots that were taking place at the University of Mississippi (Ole Miss) and she was angry that the school was being forced to integrate. Much to Mother's dismay, her speech was peppered with the word "n*****."

Eventually, my mother had enough and told Mrs. Robins that she did not agree with her racial views. Mrs. Robins' immediate retort was to ask what my mother would do if one of her children married a "n*****." My mother replied that she would, of course, be worried for their safety, but if they loved each other and understood the difficulties, she would be happy to have a Negro woman in her family. Mrs. Robins found my mother's response unbelievably obscene and never spoke to her again.

~ ~ ~

---

[17] Over the years, I have asked a number of white friends from those days if they knew the name of Mrs. Robins' servant. No one, including myself, knew his name.

By now, I was seeing and understanding Jim Crow with increased frequency. I was not a witness to the next incident, but my dad told me this story. Since it took place at my friend Richard Jones' house, at a location I knew, I remember it as if I were there.

The Jones house had front, side, and back entrances. Because of the layout, it was not easy to tell which door was the back entrance and which was the side. Probably by mistake, a Black man had gone to the side door of Mr. Jones' house. Black people were supposed to go to the back door, *never, **never*** the side or front door. The man knocked and when Mr. Jones came to the door and saw a Black man, he flew into a rage. He stormed out of the house, hitting the man and knocking him to the ground. Cursing and yelling, Mr. Jones ran into his house to get his gun with the intention of returning to kill the Black man.

Fortunately, the man was able to run away, but if my friend's father had succeeded in shooting the man, I question if there would have been serious consequences. In all likelihood, the Black man did not realize he was at the wrong door. In DeWitt everyone, Black and white, knew the rules of behavior and the sometimes deadly consequences to Black people for breaking those rules. Whether the decree was broken intentionally or unintentionally was of no importance.

My father knew that if I heard this from friends, Mr. Jones would be thought of as a hero for standing up to the "uppity n*****." The terror that the Black man must have experienced would be something for my peers to laugh at. Dad wanted me to hear the story from him.

Later, after I had thought about it, I told my dad that I thought Mr. Jones must be a bad man.

"A person can be a good person but be wrong in the way he conducts one area of his life," Dad told me. "Mr. Jones is not all bad, but he is very wrong when he treats Negroes that way."

I treated Mr. Jones with respect because I was not allowed to disrespect any adult. However, I never was able to separate the good from the evil.

~ ~ ~

In 1963, the year I turned thirteen years old, there was no Civil Rights Movement in DeWitt, Arkansas. The very phrase "civil rights" was seldom spoken, and when it was, it took on a different meaning from today. Today, the term means equal rights, but at that time, it was used in reference to the legal system.

For a Black person to speak out in favor of civil rights in the rural South was dangerous. My peers frequently told me how their parents had asked their Black servants what they thought of civil rights, or desegregation. The answer was always the same. "You treat me and my family good. I don't like this desegregation; it ain't right. We like to be to ourselves." Black people who answered in this manner, and in DeWitt it seemed that they all did, that person were referred to as a "good n*****."

In rural areas such as DeWitt, any progress toward equality would have to come through new laws and the enforcement of those laws. The economic hold of segregation on rural Black people was too great and the consequences to one's family and person too dangerous for any grassroots movement.

Southerners commonly believed that the Civil Rights Movement was an attack on their way of life. Whenever we heard news of demonstrations in other parts of the state, rumors that Black people were coming to DeWitt quickly followed. On one occasion, a bus with tinted windows came into town. The dark windows caused the passengers to look more Black than white, so the word spread throughout town that a busload of "colored people" was at the town square to demonstrate. In spite of the short time it took to check out the rumor, the word of the impending demonstration spread faster.

As soon as the bus stopped and white people stepped off, it was clear that demonstrations were not coming to town on that day. The tension quickly deescalated, but people in the town remained in a high state of alert. This was the atmosphere of DeWitt in 1963.

It Is Hate That Kills

Two events in 1963 further strengthened my parents' conviction that racial discrimination was wrong. The first was on August 28, 1963, when Dr. Martin Luther King, Jr., gave his "I Have a Dream" speech. His vision for America, so eloquently spoken, moved both my parents.

Dad was particularly struck by King's words about his dream for his own and other children.

> *I have a dream that my four little children will one day live in a nation where they will not be judged by the color of their skin but by the content of their character.*
>
> *I have a dream today.*
>
> *I have a dream that one day, down in Alabama, with its vicious racists, with its governor having his lips dripping with the words of interposition and nullification; one day right there in Alabama, little black boys and black girls will be able to join hands with little white boys and white girls as sisters and brothers.*

Neither of my parents remember talking to anyone other than each other about the speech and King's words. What would be the use? Dr. King was a hated man among most white people in DeWitt.

At the time of the speech, John Fitzgerald Kennedy was president, and most white people in DeWitt hated him as much as King. The Civil Rights Movement was moving forward in the larger cities and towns of the South, and Kennedy was seen as one of the architects who threatened Jim Crow.

To my knowledge, no African American person in DeWitt dared speak publicly in support of King, Kennedy, or any person working for integration. White people who spoke out could be placing themselves in harm's way and subjecting themselves to loss of jobs, economic sanctions, and the possibility of a violent assault. But the worse forms of violence were usually reserved for Black people, their families, and their communities.

The second defining event happened on Friday, November 22, 1963, when President Kennedy was shot and killed in Dallas, Texas. Dad was returning home by bus from Washington D.C. with a group of church leaders when they stopped at Thomas Jefferson's home, Monticello, and noticed the flag at half-staff. One of the riders asked a staff member why the flag was lowered. He answered, "The president is dead." Thinking this must be in commemoration of some historical event, it took a while for the news to sink in. The unthinkable had happened, and the long bus ride to Arkansas was a solemn and painful trip.

Mother was talking to Ruby Hampton, a friend from church, when they heard it being broadcast on the television. Their thoughts were the same as those returning from Washington D.C. — a horror that was unimaginable only moments earlier had taken place.

When the announcement was made on the school intercom, my brother, Ron was sitting in a seventh-grade class that cheered. I was sitting in eighth-grade science, and when our class heard the announcement all reacted in shocked silence. The bell rang and I stepped into the hall to see one boy walking down the corridor yelling in celebration, "They finally got that n*****-lover."

In shock, I shuffled into the next class, math with Mrs. Davis.

"Are we going to discuss President Kennedy's assassination?" one of the girls asked.

"You will hear enough about that when you get home," Mrs. Davis answered. She then proceeded to teach us math. I don't remember a thing about her lesson, but I do remember her seeming indifference to the death of the president of our country.

Thirteen-year-old boys aren't known to cry much in public, but it was all I could do to keep from breaking down until I got home.

Walking home on a beautiful autumn day, I usually thought about the upcoming weekend, which would consist of playing sandlot football until it became too dark to see, going out to visit one of my friends on his farm, church on Sunday morning and evening, and participating in whatever else the weekend might have to offer. On this day, I wasn't thinking of the football games or the weekend ahead. I was mourning the death of the president, and I felt different and utterly alone.

As soon as I entered our home, I burst into tears. I told Mother about the boy cheering the assassination. But Mother explained to me in words I understood why that boy was wrong and why our family does not use that word nor do we cheer at the murder that had just taken place.

In town, the initial jubilation of a few gave way to universal mourning. Although the announcement that President

Kennedy was shot is still etched in my mind, my memories of the days following his death are spotty.

Two days after the assassination, Lee Harvey Oswald, the alleged assassin, was shot and killed on live TV as he was being transferred to a different jail. I asked my father if he thought Oswald would go to heaven. In uncharacteristic anger, Dad, who taught us that God loved everyone and that we would all end up with God, said he didn't think Oswald would make it. I remember the funeral procession and the slow, measured cadence of the drums. The entire nation was in mourning. What is most imprinted in my mind is the sadness.

Two days passed, and it was Sunday, November 24, 1963. The weather, as I recall, was clear and cool. In times of crisis, the rural South looks to its faith, and on that day the churches were filled. Dad had preached against segregation from the day we arrived in DeWitt, but his sermons were subtle. If someone chose to overlook the deeper meaning of the sermons, he or she could do so. That Sunday the title of the sermon was "It Is Hate That Kills" and it spoke directly to segregation and racial bigotry.

Reverend McDonald told of his trip from Washington D.C. and quoted from a newspaper he bought along the way. Phil Sullivan in an editorial for the *Nashville Tennessean* wrote, "Innocent children have been dynamited in Sunday School. We have grown used to seeing on television and in the news pictures the hate-twisted faces of young men and woman as well as adults crying out the most violent threats and expressing a virulence of venom against their country and its authority. ...

"So, at this hour, before we begin to mourn, we would do well to understand that hate can kill a President, and if unchecked on behalf of morality, decency and human dignity it can kill a nation or so weaken it that it will die."

No longer quoting the editorial – and speaking symbolically – my father said, "Who killed President Kennedy? I suppose you could say we all are a part of the slaying. I helped kill the President when I did not and do not speak out against hate. We might as well face it. The racial problems that confront us are stirred up by hate. Hate will not solve any problem, much less the problem of living together as brothers."

The message of his sermon was that racial bigotry and hate were wrong. This time, the message was not subtle. It could not be overlooked.

When Bishop Pope had first spoken to Dad almost three years earlier about moving to DeWitt, Dad had known a time would come when he would feel compelled to speak out against racism. When that happened, he knew there would be trouble. The moment had arrived and things could no longer go on in the same way. Sitting in the church and listening to my father's sermon, I knew that something important was taking place. I wonder if my father fully understood the significance of the sermon he was preaching. When John Fitzgerald Kennedy was murdered, my father heard the shots and his faith told him he must speak against the hate and prejudice that permeated his community. My father had thrown down the gauntlet and it could not be taken back.

When speaking out against racism, my father stepped over the line of acceptable behavior, but the communities' collective pain seemed to have drained everyone of energy. Friends told me about other services in other churches. No one, at least in the white churches, spoke on race relations. My father's sermon passed with little comment. It would be several months before the segregationists would respond.

The assassination took a toll on the emotional life of our town, as it did with the entire nation. President Kennedy had been disliked and often hated by the white citizens of town, but the people of DeWitt were not prepared for the actual assassination of the president. Our country's sense of security was taken away.

After President Kennedy's death and my father's sermon, the town and the church took some time to reflect and regroup. Much of life in farming communities was governed by the change of season. Fields had to be plowed and then planted. The crops had to be tended and, when it was time, harvested. Hunting season was strictly regulated and began in the late fall and continued through the winter – after harvest and before planting. "For everything there is a season," and after the assassination, the season was late fall and early winter. DeWitt took solace in hunting, Thanksgiving, and Christmas.

~ ~ ~

The funeral home for white people was run by the Essex family, and they were avid duck hunters. Jack Essex was also chairman of the Official Board at the church. He had two sons old enough to go hunting, and they went at every opportunity. The Essex family rules of operation only allowed three reasons for not hunting: they would not hunt when there was a death – business reasons; they would not hunt on Christmas day – marital reasons (Mrs. Essex wouldn't allow it); and they would not hunt on Sunday during church–religious reasons. They would go early Sunday morning, but they were always back in time to dress for Sunday school and church. Another reason to not hunt would not exactly be classified as a rule but was rather a dictate from Mr. Essex himself: "Never go hunting with a game warden." I will leave it up to the reader to determine why Jack Essex felt it necessary to issue that order.

Dad didn't actively pursue wild game a lot but he did enjoy duck hunting. When he went, it was almost always with the Essex family. My brother Ron and I were old enough to go along, and when Dad went on school days, he would take one of us. Those times were rare, but they are the trips I recall fondly.

On our trips before school, Dad would wake me up while it was still dark. We would get into our clothes, grab some breakfast, and as quickly as possible head out to the woods, with my school clothes stashed away in the car. A small group of hunters would assemble at a designated location, usually on the edge of a farm field. Rice that did not make it into the Harvester was scattered throughout the flooded fields and attracted water fowl. The duck blind, our destination, was only accessible by foot, which meant walking through the water. We wore hip boots to keep dry. The only socks I owned were cotton, and I would wear two pairs, but that did little to keep out the bone-chilling temperature of the water. Ice-cold feet were an unavoidable part of the experience in those days.

The surface under the water was uneven, muddy, and littered with tree roots and fallen branches. To take a fall was normal, especially for kids, and that meant being drenched in the ice-cold water and becoming increasingly cold and uncomfortable. There was no turning back because of a spill, but there was one consideration given to the unlucky souls that took in water. Those who fell were allowed to take off their hip boots and pour out the water when we reached the duck blind.

The dogs that would retrieve the ducks always had the time of their lives romping and swimming through the water. I would be struggling not to fall, afraid of the cold water, while the dogs were bounding through the bayou, seemingly impervious to the temperature.

The duck blinds were built like camouflaged baseball dugouts, and when we reached our blind, everyone found a seat along the bench with shotguns at the ready. The idea was for each hunter to be positioned so he could stand and shoot in one smooth, quick motion. The water in front of the blind was stocked with decoys, floating imitations of ducks, and when there was enough light for the ducks to see, they would begin searching for new locations to land.

As soon as ducks were sighted, the "callers" went into action, imitating the sound of surface ducks communicating to those in flight. That responsibility fell to the Essex boys, and they used a duck caller, a three-inch-long instrument a little like a sawed-off clarinet. As the ducks came closer, the callers changed from a loud quacking to a cackling sound. No one could move or look up, but we had to be poised and ready to shoot. If the ducks were to see the whites of our eyes, so to speak, they wouldn't come toward us. Movements as subtle as the reflection of a metal buckle could spook the ducks. Just like the humans, the dogs were trained to remain motionless. On one of my first trips, I looked up and a flock of ducks went from landing to flying away. The experienced hunters became detectives, trying to figure out what went wrong. I fessed up. Everyone was very polite when they told me I should not do that again, but the message was clear. I kept my gaze down after that. It was considered poor sportsmanship to shoot a sitting duck, so when the ducks were near but still in flight the callers would yell to us that we could fire. "Take 'em!" they would shout.

Once, I was the only one to shoot in one direction and I got an undisputable kill. Dad looked at me and nodded. "You got that duck," he said. I was on top of the world. In about a minute, we went from sitting motionless, to standing and shooting, to sending the dogs out to retrieve the kill. After the dogs retrieved the ducks, we would settle back and look for other flocks in flight. This routine was repeated until we reached our legal limit or until it was time to go to school.

When it was time to leave, we would walk back through the water to the vehicles, where I got in the car and changed into my school clothes as Dad drove to the school. Then I laid my feet on the car heater, trying to warm my toes enough so I could walk without pain. Dad would drop me off at school, then he would go home, change, and go to work. Those early morning excursions were cold, uncomfortable, and tiring — but great adventures. I no longer hunt, but when I look back to those trips, they are among my favorite childhood memories.

~ ~ ~

As winter ended, farmers took to the fields. The workload got heavy and they would work from sun-up to sundown, so if the segregationists were to confront my father, they would need to do it soon. It was now common knowledge where Dad stood on race relations. Had my father been Black, his life would have been in danger. If he was being threatened, I never knew it, but it was not a good time for anyone who opposed Jim Crow. Separation of the races was being challenged throughout the South, and white people were living in fear that it would also be confronted in DeWitt. In an attempt to integrate places of worship, there was a group of African American college students from Pine Bluff who were attending white churches around the state. Considering my father's views, it was correctly assumed that if those students came to our place of worship, they would be seated.

However, the test to the policy of the First Methodist Church in DeWitt did not come from Black college students. It came from its members. In the winter of 1964, the segregationists decided that they would take their stand at an Official Board meeting, the governing body of each Methodist church. At a February meeting of the Board, it was proposed that if a Black person were to come into the church, he or she would not be seated but directed to one of the town's African American churches. It is ironic that this resolution was introduced on a date designated by the national body of the Methodist Church as "Race Relations Sunday." In the discussion that ensued it became apparent that the one person who could overrule a Board vote was prepared to do so. That individual was my father.

Board members on both sides of the issue loved their place of worship and rather than risk a separation they might not be able to repair, it was decided that the resolution would be tabled until the following month.

That night, my parents gathered my four brothers and me around the kitchen table. They told us what happened at the Board meeting and explained that because of the conflict there might be problems at school. My brothers and I had several questions.

We asked who made the proposal to bar Black people from the church, but Dad wouldn't tell us. I was an adult before I was to learn that one of the people was Frank Jones, the man who had threatened to kill a Black man for coming to his side door and the father of my friend and one of my brother Don's best friends. I don't know if Mr. Jones told his son, Richard, what happened with the Board, but there was never any indication that he knew and we remained friends. Frank Jones would strongly differ with my father for the entire time we were in DeWitt, but he always spoke highly of Dad.

Seated in the kitchen, one of us asked our father why he would do this, since he knew that it was going to cause so much trouble. He gave us two reasons. First, Dad said that during the Official Board meeting, he had thought of us, his children. He said he always taught us that everyone was equal and that we should never treat anyone poorly because they were Negroes. He said that now was a time when he had to practice what he preached and he would have a hard time living with himself if he didn't do what was right. His "practice what I preach" statement got a laugh. When we, the kids, caught him doing something different than what he had instructed us to do, his response was always, "Practice what I preach, not what I do."

The other reason was rooted in my parents' faith. He said that he believed Jesus would have spoken out. The church, my father believed, was for all people, and he could not remain silent when some people wanted to exclude those whose skin color was different than ours.

My brother, Ron and I are the only ones of the McDonald boys old enough to remember that meeting around the kitchen table. DeWitt was a small town and the Official Board meeting was a major event, so there was no doubt that news of the meeting would be all over town in short order. Ron and I were also the only ones with peers old enough to understand that there was a fight over allowing Black people to attend our Methodist church. That night I fell asleep wondering what my friends would have to say at school the next day.

In the morning at school, there was a chill in my interactions with a few of my acquaintances. The son of a member of the Official Board attacked me, but the damage wasn't too great. He was older, bigger, and faster than me, and I had the good sense to stay down without a fight. His father strongly opposed Dad, and the attack seemed out of nowhere. I had no idea if I was attacked because he disliked me or if he was angry with my father. I never discussed the Official Board meeting or my father's views on race with any of my peers.

Ron, on the other hand, did not fare so well. His best friend's father was a leader of the anti-segregation group that brought the resolution to the Official Board, and his friend's brother was the very same young man who had attacked me. Ron was shunned by his friends, on occasion physically attacked, and became an outcast among his peers for the remainder of our time in DeWitt.

~ ~ ~

February and March of 1964 were a busy time for Dad. He questioned the system of segregation that had been unchanged for the lifetime of every member of the church congregation. Several wanted to talk to Dad and hear what he had to say. Others just wanted to tell him how much they disagreed with his views on race.

Dad wanted to talk to members of his congregation, too. If the vote were to go against him, he had the right to override the Board's decision, but it would come at a cost. At best, it would divide the church.

One didn't have to look far to see a worst-case scenario. Pine Bluff was the next county over and only fifty-eight miles from DeWitt. It was close enough that when the wind blew from the west to the east, the sour, unpleasant odor from Pine Bluff's paper mills passed through DeWitt. Pine Bluff was the larger of the two communities and the home of what we refer to these days as an HBCU (historically Black college or university). Because of Pine Bluff's size, the college, and the large Black population, white people in the city were hypervigilant in their attempt to stop integration. Pine Bluff also had an organized white resistance to integration.

On the same day that the motion was made to bar Black people from the church in DeWitt, the Reverend Edward W. Harris at the First Methodist Church in Pine Bluff gave a sermon in support of integration. In front of his congregation, Harris said, "The Church must work to change those community patterns in which racial segregation appears, including education, housing, voting, employment, and the use of public facilities." Harris had also thrown out the gauntlet.

The white community's response to Harris was immediate and harsh. While Dad was trying to keep his church from being divided, Harris and his family were living with a bombardment of threats. They could not allow their daughter to answer the phone because of the constant death threats they were receiving. The continued heated response and lack of support from the Arkansas Methodist leadership forced the

Harris family to move.[18] The stakes for those who took a stand were high.

~ ~ ~

As the grown-ups were debating the issue of race, I also experienced my own inner conflict. Every day, Dad came home for lunch. If the meal was not ready, he went into the kitchen to help my mother and discussed what had transpired during the morning. On this day, Dad was in the kitchen assisting with the last-minute preparations and talking to Mother. They did not know I was listening.

"I've been reading about George Wallace," he said.

George Wallace, a former progressive on the issue of race relations, was the governor of Alabama, and like several other southern governors, was making a name for himself opposing integration. Few could equal the hate-filled and racist rhetoric that came from the mouth of this Alabama governor.

Dad told Mother that he believed Wallace was "fanning the flames of hatred" all over the South and he believed Wallace was making it difficult for those working for integration.

Then Dad said something that would influence the entire direction of my life. "If something happens to me, George Wallace bears some of the responsibility."

Up until that moment, I knew what Dad was doing and I believed in it. I thought of it as some kind of conflict that would resolve itself in time. It had never occurred to me that there were risks.

---

[18] Clemons and Farr, *Crisis of Conscience*, 187–191.

With those words, I understood for the first time that what was happening to my father could be dangerous. He could be hurt – or killed.

I thoroughly enjoyed my life in DeWitt, but the very people that I saw as friends could be the people who would harm my father. To my horror, the danger could also come from the church, a place both my parents and I loved. I was totally and utterly terrified.[19]

~ ~ ~

After a tense month, the Board met. Official Board meetings were normally routine and enjoyable events. People discussed the nuts and bolts of running an organization they cared deeply for.

This meeting had more the feel of people entering battle. The resolution to bar Black people was on the agenda and the tension was high. If the resolution passed, Dad would overrule the majority and some members would leave the church in protest. If the resolution failed and the church was opened to anyone, of any race, those same members would leave.

---

[19] The strange thing is that today I do not know if Dad actually said that last sentence about George Wallace. He may have said it, or it might have come from my imagination. My adolescent brain may have added that sentence into their conversation as a way to put into words my increased understanding of the risk my father was taking. Whether the words were spoken or imagined, they have stayed with me as I struggled to come to terms in my relationship with the South, Arkansas, DeWitt, the Church, and God.

Either way, the First Methodist Church in DeWitt would probably be divided.

The meeting was called to order by the chair, Jack Essex. Before anyone could speak, one board member, Barnes Hampton, stood.

"Mr. Chairman, I move we adjourn," he said.

"I second it," board member Pat Pattillo said.

"We have a motion and a second. All in favor?" Jack Essex said.

"Aye," said the vast majority.

"All opposed."

"Nay," said a few members.

"Meeting adjourned."

Within a few seconds, the Official Board meeting was over. The message to those determined to have a stated policy of segregation was clear. While the majority may or may not have supported integration, they would not allow the issue to tear the church apart. The motion to bar Black people would not be brought to the floor again. The crisis that would have split the church was averted.

Three men — Barnes Hampton, Jack Essex, and Pat Pattillo — had, without my father's knowledge, hatched this strategy to save the church, and it worked. Realizing the motion would not be voted on at this or any other Official Board meeting, the father of Ron's former best friend and of the boy who beat me up stormed out, never to return.

The resolution was dead, but if a Black person had shown up for worship, he or she would still not be welcomed. Dad immediately went to work on his own, taking steps to ensure that no one would be turned away. He went to each of the ushers and asked if they were willing to seat a Black person. If they were not willing, then they were very tactfully replaced. All were told that if a Black person were to attend the church, they should be seated with my family.

This was no small issue. While there were a number of people willing to allow Black people to worship in the church, there could have been trouble if the visitors were seated in the same pew with some members. It would have been especially troublesome to have a Black man next to a white woman. Having a Black person in a pew with our family would be breaking one more of society's rules by placing a racially mixed group together. The other option would be to follow the custom and have the Black individuals sit at the very back and separate from all the white people, but that my father was not going to allow. Placing the individuals with my family was a surefire way to ensure that there would be no protest from the white people seated in the same pew. My mother strongly supported integration of the races and she would not only allow Black to sit with her family, she would welcome them.

Since no Black person ever attended our church while we were there, we would never know how the church and community would react. Even so, tensions still simmered and a few people would no longer speak to my family or me.

I Was Scared to Death

In preparation for Annual Conference, the local Pastor Staff Committee met to decide whether to recommend to the bishop whether my father stayed or moved. The congregation did not have the power to fire someone because they did not approve of his views. The bishop was the only person who could officially reassign an individual to another church and during the civil rights days, that was significant.

Even though the Pastor Staff Committee had no power on paper, its recommendation was given strong consideration by the bishop. The Pastor Staff Committee requested that Dad remain in DeWitt.

Since Bishop Pope was an integrationist, Dad did not have to worry about his job. No other church clergy in DeWitt was publicly supporting integration. In the white churches, that was probably in part due to fear of being dismissed by the congregation for speaking out. Bishop Pope agreed with the committee's recommendation and agreed that the McDonalds should remain. My parents liked DeWitt and were happy with the decision.

By Sunday, May 24, 1964, the bishop's official decision that our father would stay in DeWitt was made and the changes to allow Black entry into church were in place. Dad was free to announce the news to the church congregation.

Sunday's worship service began as it always did, with the opening music, prayers, and rituals. Reverend McDonald started the sermon with the announcement that we were reassigned to DeWitt. Then he said he believed it was time to address some issues he saw as central to the church's future.

He spoke of his belief that Christianity was a faith rooted in love and relayed his conviction that it was an inclusive faith, not an exclusive set of beliefs.

He said, "We have liked everywhere we have lived. We have enjoyed every church we have been privileged to serve in. But I can say with all sincerity that we have enjoyed living and working here more than any other church and community. Lois and I have talked about this time and time again. Our family was accepted in a marvelous way, but I am sure some wondered about a preacher with five boys."

Then my father took up the issue of race.

"For over two months now we have been discussing the race problem as it affects our church. I am quite sure you all know my convictions and beliefs, and so I do not believe that it is necessary for me to discuss them now.

"I have tried since I have been your pastor to lift up what I feel to be the gospel of Jesus Christ as it is related to the social problems we are facing today. I realize, of course, that not everyone agreed with me, but I felt and still feel that I must, as a preacher of the gospel, try to follow Jesus. I have tried to do this with love, for without love, nothing can be done. I have not tried to force my beliefs on those who disagree, but at the same time I have hoped to lead them.

"We can't stop the world and get off," my father said. "We are living in an age of revolution and change and as Christians, church people, we must react as Jesus would have us react.

"Maybe it is good that we have faced this problem, and I am sure that it is far from solved. But I am convinced that we have spent enough time discussing this problem.

"I must confess I have prayed more about this than any problem I have faced in my ministry. I have discussed it sometimes, it seems, night and day. I have spent many sleepless hours thinking about it, and I hope that I have a better understanding of the problem. I know I feel closer to God and I have felt His leadership.

"I have felt the strength of others — of friends and my own family."

The sermon then took a change in direction. He spoke of the reverence he had felt for church since childhood.

"We are gathered here in the Lord's house. This is a holy and hallowed place. Much has taken place here. We were baptized, joined the church here, some were married here, our loved ones have been buried from here."

Dad asked the congregation to reflect on a series of queries about how we treat others and how our faith is practiced, then closed with a prayer.

"I need to ask God to forgive me and help me to look up — and love — and lift.

"God, I need thee every hour. Now and in these moments we all need thee to lead us on in the greater work of thy Church that we might help build the Kingdom of God.

"Fill us ... mold us ... make us ... use us ... in Christ's Service."

Several times Dad repeated his belief that Jesus would welcome all people into any place of worship. My father's profound belief that the church was for *all* people was the recurrent theme throughout his sermon. Today, the words sound inspirational but mild, but in South Arkansas in 1964, they were enormously powerful. My father said things that had never been spoken from the pulpit of a white church in DeWitt.

Normally during church, I sat in the back with my friends, fidgeting, passing notes, and playing tic-tac-toe, but this time was different. I was glued to every word. Racial jokes had been told in the church's corridors and classrooms. I had frequently sat in Sunday School classes feeling isolated from my peers while listening to teachers and peers justify bigotry using biblical passages. Now my father was saying, from the pulpit, that the racism, bigotry, and hate that oozed into every aspect of our lives were wrong. I had taken on my parents' beliefs as my own, and I no longer had to feel that I was an alien because I believed in those principles.

When the sermon ended, my father looked at the congregation. He realized that he didn't want to stand at the sanctuary door, shake hands, and engage in casual conversation. He suspected many at the service felt the same. He then did something he had not planned. He said, "You're dismissed," and walked out. There was no closing song or benediction.

During his more than sixty years of leading worship services, that was the only time he ever walked out. People sat in the pews, stunned, and confused. It seemed like an eternity before they stood and began to leave the church. Few spoke and no one stood at the doors as the congregation left. Everyone went to their cars and drove away.

When the service was over, my brother Ron rushed back to Dad's office to see him supporting himself against his desk. The Board chair, Jack Essex, then came into my father's office and spoke to him. Ron slipped away without hearing what was said, but as an adult, Ron asked Dad what he was thinking when he was leaning on his desk. Dad said, "I was scared to death." At the time, I didn't know my father was afraid. I thought he was the most courageous person alive.

~ ~ ~

Following the sermon, a change took place in the church and with the congregation. Resistance to my father diminished and then virtually disappeared. If someone had tried to integrate the church, the conflict would surely have resurfaced, but that did not happen. Instead, the church experienced one of its most successful years ever. Pledges increased dramatically and by the end of year, the church was on very sound financial ground. The few who had left in protest were replaced by a surge in membership.

One year later, we left DeWitt. Frank Jones, the man who wanted to attack a Black man for coming to the side door of his house, never agreed with Dad on the issue of race. Before we moved to Rogers, Arkansas, however, Jones met with members of our next church and spoke highly of Dad. Jones said he did not see eye-to-eye with my father on every issue but that he was a good man and good preacher. My father always considered Frank Jones a friend.

The Pastor Staff Committee again recommended that our family remain in DeWitt for another year, but the bishop wanted Dad to serve in a different church.

Epilogue

~

My Parents' Legacy

Life's funny. In the first half of the twentieth century, before Charles McDonald and Lois King knew each other, they came to know people of color long before those experiences were remotely common or acceptable. After they married and had a family, their experiences from the 1940s helped them to take a stand in the 1960s. When my father preached about equality and justice, others took these values into their own lives to go on to influence others.

In 2023, my parents have six living sons. Only two of their children were old enough to remember the time in DeWitt, and one was not yet born at that time, but the experience still influences all our lives. That core belief in the equality of all people, taught by my parents and then my brothers, has passed to the third and fourth generation. My nephews, nieces, and my own son are caring, compassionate people who are teaching their children these values. I am proud.

For years I have been fascinated with the question of why people stand up for what they believe is right when it carries no personal benefits. Why do ordinary people take extraordinary risk? Many years ago, I read that those who hid Jews from the Nazis were usually people who fit in well into their community and were not known as rabble-rousers. They were not looking for a cause. When asked why they did what they did, their most frequent response was that they did not believe what was happening to the Jews was right and they were compelled to act.

Mahatma Gandhi was an attorney by profession yet chose a life devoted to a cause. Dr. Martin Luther King, Jr., lived in the Jim Crow South but because of his fairly economically and educationally privileged status, he did not have to suffer the worst of segregation. Nevertheless, he took a stand for justice and, for that, he paid with his life. My own parents had a position of status in the towns they served, but they spoke out against injustice despite personal risk.

Every generation has those who are willing to take extraordinary risks for their beliefs. For many, the principles are rooted in their religious faith; others simply do what they believe is right. It seems to me that in spite of the differences, these people carry with them a common set of principles. Those principles are rooted in a core belief in the humanity and interconnection of all people.

History shows us that the people who act on their convictions are, like all of us, often plagued with troubles in other areas of their life. They aren't perfect; they are human. Still, they understand that there are times when one must speak out.

~ ~ ~

In August 2012, my parents were visited by Belinda Snow, a Black woman who was a family friend. We watched a DVD that was made by the Central High School National Historic Site about Dad's involvement in the Civil Rights Movement. Dad was very sick, and they both knew they were seeing each other for the last time. Belinda rose and joked about kissing Dad on his bald head. She did, and we all laughed.

"I want to thank you for what you did," she whispered in his ear.

Tears came to Dad's eyes and his voice shook when he answered. "I wish I had done more."

I thought Dad was referring to the times he stayed quiet when he witnessed something evil – events like watching a Black man being forced to stand in the mud so that two white men could pass on the high and dry walkway or listening to racist jokes and comments while remaining silent. Unlike Dad, I was thinking about the pride I felt for the times he spoke out.

The moment passed quickly and when she left, we were again laughing.

Before his death, Dad told me that he was ashamed because he had done so little in support of the Civil Rights struggle. He believed he should have attended some of the national demonstrations but he did not because he was afraid.

I have spent much time wondering if my father should have done more in support for the cause and I do not know. It may come down to what my brother, Tom, wrote about our dad.

"During the Civil Rights Movement of the 1950s and 1960s, there were men and women like Daisy Bates and Martin Luther King who created tidal waves by their work and their deeds. Then there were others, like my father, who created ripples. Those ripples may not seem like much to some people, but to this white boy growing up in the turbulent South, they were the difference between right and wrong."

On September 6, 2012, Dad passed away. He died exactly the way he wanted to – surrounded by those he loved, his humor intact, and engaged with others to the end. His memorial service overflowed with people from many backgrounds, other countries, and various races and religions. Dad would have liked that.

Less than two years later, my mother died. She was at peace with death. Like Dad, Mother's service was full, and many there told us of the positive influence she had in their lives. Lois Lee King McDonald was a life well lived.

Decades ago in DeWitt, Arkansas, a town of barely three thousand people, a Methodist minister and his wife stood up for what they believed, and I was privileged to have a front-row seat. When all the rhetoric is put aside, they took the position they did for the simple reason that they believed it was the right thing to do. No TV cameras or reporters were present. No movie scripts were written about these events, and what happened never made it into history books. For my parents, staying silent to the injustice was too great a burden to bear. So, they spoke out against hate and inequality, and because of that, our world is a better place.

Appendix

~

Where Are They Now?

DR. JULIUS SCOTT, JR.

Julius Scott was the African American man Dad roomed with in Michigan in 1945. Through the years, Dad followed his former roommate's successful career. Sixty-four years after their time in Michigan, Dr. Scott was the interim president of Philander Smith College, the headquarters of the Arkansas United Methodist Church. One afternoon, after conducting some business at the church headquarters, Mother and Dad decided to pay him a visit.

After introductions, Dad told Dr. Scott, "I don't know if you remember, but I roomed with you in 1945. When I arrived at the conference and realized that I would be rooming with an African American, I was, at first, upset. I was never around Black people. My next thought was, 'I am a Christian at a Christian gathering and it isn't right to refuse to room with someone because of the color of his skin.' When we roomed together, I came to understand that just because a person is Black, it doesn't mean they are less than me. You were the most popular person there and you were clearly more talented than me in many ways. That experience affected my life and because of that experience, I made the decision to pursue equality between the races aggressively throughout my career.

"I have followed your career through the years and when I heard you were here, I wanted to see you."

Julius Scott looked my father in the eye and said, "Charles, you were the first white man I ever roomed with." They both laughed.

My white father, my white mother, and this Black man spent time together. They talked of their experiences at the church conference in 1945, they talked about the church and what it meant to them, they talked about race relations, and they talked about their lives. Sixty years earlier the conversation they were having could not have openly taken place in Arkansas. They laughed and enjoyed each other's company.

Dr. Scott died in 2019.

The Pocahontas Colored School

While writing this book, I have had the opportunity to talk to several people who played a key role in my parents' life. One of the most rewarding experiences happened when I talked to a colleague and friend, the Reverend Freddie Smith. Freddie comes from a town roughly 250 miles from Pocahontas. Outside of family and very close friends, I do not recall ever telling anyone about Dad's encounters with Miss Eddie Mae Herron McDonald, the Pocahontas Colored School teacher who told Dad about her class trip to the Memphis Zoo.

For some reason I told Freddie. When I finished, Freddie said, "You are not going to believe this, but the Pocahontas Colored School is now a museum and my son volunteers there." The museum is named the Eddie Mae Herron Center after the very woman who talked to my father in 1949, forty-eight years earlier.

On August 20, 2007, after a series of emails and phone calls to Freddie's son, Frederick, I learned that Miss Eddie Mae had been the only teacher at the Pocahontas Colored School. She died a few years after civil rights legislation forced the Pocahontas School District to integrate and was buried at the Haven of Rest Cemetery in Little Rock.

I also learned that there were some people in Pocahontas who wanted to meet us. On a hot August day, I drove my parents there. We arrived at the Herron Center to find a small crowd of people. Two of those meeting us were passengers on the bus to the Memphis Zoo. Others were there because they heard we would be meeting and they wanted to be a witness to the event. Several remembered my parents, and old friendships were renewed.

There were white and Black people, and they ranged in age from a nineteen-year-old Black college student to a 100-year-old white woman. We looked around the museum and enjoyed each other's company in what was almost a carnival atmosphere. Then we took our seats around the room. Once seated, each person shared.

My dad talked about Miss Eddie Mae and how she and her friendship impacted him. "It encouraged me and strengthened me to be an advocate all of my life for integration, in the church, in the schools, in all of Arkansas. It really had an impact on my life. I always remembered her as a person of real compassion and real concern for the children and what happened that day."

Mrs. Ruth Newman was a chaperone and mother of two of the children on the bus. She told how that day was "a bad time, a real bad time." She stated that a group of white people gathered around them at Overton Park, seemingly waiting for the police to arrive. When they did show up, two officers came out of the car cursing and threatening the group. One man was waving his club in the air, sending a frightening message that he was prepared to begin beating any member of the group. Miss Eddie Mae and Mrs. Newman frantically loaded the children on the bus while Mr. Rex Harper, the white bus driver, attempted to calm the enforcers. Again, and again Mr. Harper said that the incident was a "misunderstanding," but the men in blue wouldn't listen. While the Memphis police threatened the school group, the all-white crowd stood and watched. No person lifted a finger or spoke in protest about what they were witnessing.

As the bus was finally driving away, the children kept asking the adults, "What did we do wrong?"

I asked Mrs. Newman how the adults explained what happened to the students on the bus. She said they did not discuss the event at all. If they allowed the boys and girls to talk about what happened, they might get angry with the oppressors and their anger could grow into rage, which could lead them to protest segregation. To protest segregation could be dangerous. Children needed to accept the way things were and move on.

Mrs. Newman taught her own children about segregation. She taught them to know their place. It was the law, and to remain safe, her children had to accept the reality and conform. Mrs. Newman and her late husband told their children that it was all about skin color. Their skin was black, the others' skin was white, and they had to stay away from those with white skin.

"I have been scared of Memphis ever since," she said.

My mother, Lois, told how Miss Eddie Mae influenced the direction of her husband's ministry and how it strengthened their resolve to teach their children to be accepting of people of different races and religions. Many of Mother's children and grandchildren took on beliefs that were different from her own, but she said she believed they respect all people, regardless of their differences.

My brother Ron was also there. He remembered the time Dad preached in the commencement service at the Pocahontas Colored School. Ron talked about his reactions to attending his first Black service. After the commencement address and on the ride home, Ron referred to the custom of "call and response," speaking words of encouragement and agreement to the pastor's sermon. Ron asked our dad why people talked while he was preaching. Dad told Ron that was the way the preacher knew the congregation was paying attention.

As we chuckled at Dad's explanation, Ron added, "I'm glad people didn't speak during Dad's sermons in our church. If they did, Dad would have known I wasn't paying attention." It was one of many lighter moments.

I talked about being able to meet and listen to some of the people who were on the bus to Memphis and how special that was. I didn't say what I was really thinking because I was afraid I would break down. I believed that I was experiencing a sacred event. I was honored to sit in the building that had once been called the Pocahontas Colored School and meet and listen to people who had been on the bus, but it was also a disturbing experience. Without knowing it, I was troubled by the evil of that day even almost fifty years later.

Pat Findley Johnson spoke. "We knew our place. When something like that happens, what could you do? You couldn't speak up for yourself. You didn't have any rights. How could you – what were you going to do? And who were you going to go to? We had to depend on our parents to guide us in the right way."

She also talked about the remarkable journey the Memphis Zoo story itself had taken. It took many years for it to finally make it back to the Pocahontas Colored School. If Miss Eddie Mae had not talked to my dad, memory of the whole event would have died. One more lost bit of our shared past.

"I think it is healing when you can talk," Pat said. Without being aware of it, the people on the bus, my parents, and my family had been shackled by locks we never heard click. I believe there was a healing for people in the room, and on August 20, 2007, many of us shed some of those chains.

GOVERNOR GEORGE C. WALLACE

When I was young, George Wallace was a terrifying name to me. I saw him and his rhetoric as a very real danger to my parents.

In 1958, Wallace ran for governor of Alabama as a moderate on the issue of race. He lost. After the election, aide Seymore Trammell recalled Wallace saying, "Seymore, you know why I lost that governor's race? ... I was outniggered by John Patterson. And I'll tell you here and now, I will never be outn****red again."

After a successful race for governor, Wallace took the oath of office on January 14, 1963.

In his inaugural speech, Wallace said, "In the name of the greatest people that have ever trod this earth, I draw the line in the dust and toss the gauntlet before the feet of tyranny, and I say segregation now, segregation tomorrow, segregation forever."

He went on to become one of the most well-known opponents of integration. He was ruthless and seemed to support and call for violence to stop integration.

In 1972, while running for president of the United States, Wallace was gunned down by an assassin. He survived but was in a wheelchair for the remainder of his life.

In the late 1970s, Wallace announced that he was a born-again Christian and apologized to Black civil rights leaders for his past actions as a segregationist. He said that while he had once sought power and glory, he realized he needed to seek love and forgiveness. In 1979, Wallace said of his "Stand in the Schoolhouse Door," in which he attempted to block Black students from entering the University of Alabama: "I was wrong. Those days are over, and they ought to be over." He publicly asked for forgiveness from Black people.

In 1982, Wallace ran and was elected governor of Alabama again. During his final term as governor (1983–1987) he made a record number of Black appointments to state positions, including, for the first time, two Black people as members in the same cabinet.

It took me a long time to come to believe that the public figure I feared most might have changed. While I tend to believe he did change, I have spoken to people whom I deeply respect who do not buy it, but today I want to believe that George Wallace died a different man.

JOHNNY AND LOU CREE SCHALLHORN

The man who followed my father as pastor in DeWitt did not share his beliefs about racial equality. The First Methodist Church did not have anyone to preach the gospel of inclusion and no Black person came to the church in the years that followed, but if one had, he or she would probably not have been admitted. It seemed that what happened in DeWitt was meaningless to everyone except my family.

Twenty years after we lived in DeWitt, Dad attended a conference in Little Rock and ran into Johnny Schallhorn. Johnny was one of the owners of the hardware store in DeWitt. It was there that I had been allowed to go to the front of the line because of the color of my skin.

After visiting for a while, Johnny told Dad, "Years ago, I was a segregationist like everyone else I knew. I never thought there was anything wrong with it. When all that controversy happened around seating Black people in our church, I kept hearing you raise questions that made me wonder if segregation was right. You made some sense to me.

"Do you know what? I'm the mayor of DeWitt now, and we are having dialogue between Black people and white people and doing some of the most progressive things in race relations ever done in DeWitt. I want to thank you for how you helped."

Hearing this was particularly powerful for my brother Ron. Having become an outcast among his friends during his time in DeWitt, he still harbored resentments about that time and was unsuccessful in finding meaning from those experiences.

When Dad told him about meeting Johnny, Ron was able to put aside his resentment and replace it with a belief that good had come from our time there.

Ron now says, "No other story in my life has had such a dramatic effect upon me. In that small town I began to understand much more than church politics. I began to see the place of courage and conflict in the lives of people, and how there is a spirit that works through even the most bigoted people for eventual good."[20]

Lou Cree, who was Johnny's wife and had been Dad's secretary in DeWitt, has spent a lifetime in the service field. Ron and I recently returned to the First United Methodist Church to visit. Being around Lou Cree and Johnny was as enjoyable as when they were our babysitters in the 1960s.

THE HAMPTON FAMILY

Barnes Hampton supported my father throughout Dad's time in DeWitt. One of the people to have witnessed the racial conflict in DeWitt was Mr. Hampton's daughter, Carol. Our families stayed in touch through the years after we left town. In 1995, I was the planning chair for a Florida conference and Carol Hampton Rasco was the domestic policy advisor to President Bill Clinton. Carol was the keynote speaker, and I was scheduled to introduce her.

Before her speech, we talked about what happened in DeWitt thirty years earlier. That was the first time I had had an in-depth conversation with a peer from DeWitt about what took place.

When Carol took the podium, she spoke about my father and his stand in DeWitt. Carol said that her belief in social justice came from her family, her church, and my father. It was hard to contain the emotions I felt listening to Carol. What seemed a minor gesture in 1963 and 1964 had resonated

---

[20] Ron McDonald, *Home Again: A Pilgrimage of Father and Son* (1st Books Library: 2002), 6–8.

in the heart of a key person in the White House in 1995 and served to help support American justice.

I was always grateful to Barnes and Ruby Hampton for the support they gave my parents back in DeWitt. I believe that when the Hampton family voiced support, they helped defuse the anger directed toward my father. They were locals, not outsiders like us.

Seven years after Carol's speech in Florida, my parents and I were asked to sit at the deathbed of Ruby Hampton while her children, Carol, Martha, and Becky, came in from Washington, D.C., Little Rock, and DeWitt. Ruby and Barnes Hampton were courageous people, and I was honored to be sitting at Mrs. Hampton's bedside with members of her family. It allowed me to show, in a small way, the gratitude I felt for what the Hamptons had done for my family nearly 40 years earlier.

My father was asked to assist in Ruby Hampton's funeral and for the first time since moving from DeWitt, he spoke to many of the people who were members in the 1960s. Although we were welcomed with open arms, I had for many years built a wall of resentment for the danger my father faced in DeWitt. While seated in the sanctuary, I looked around and observed something totally different from what I had experienced in my mind. Where I had once seen people bent upon harm, I now saw people joined in concern for the Hampton family. Where I had once seen hate, I saw people united in love. Where I had once seen demons, I felt the presence of God. And the walls came tumbling down.

The congregation was still white, but an African American man came to the funeral and was seated in the middle of the sanctuary. There was a time when this one mourner would have set off untold problems, but at Mrs. Hampton's memorial service, his presence was a fitting tribute to a brave woman. I learned later that this man, Carol D'Arcy Willis, had been a longtime aide to Bill Clinton and had worked with Carol Hampton Rasco in the Arkansas Governor's Office before she went to Washington D.C. They had visited at the hospital before Ruby Hampton's death, as he had also been there with his mother. When he heard that Ruby Hampton had died, he made a point to travel to DeWitt for the service.

THE ESSEX FAMILY

The Essex family were not a group of individuals with few words. They were all blessed with the gift of gab. They also had a sense of humor that made them a joy to be around. As the owners of the funeral home, I remember Mr. Jack Essex telling me about a huge tree he had cut down and how much trouble he had finding a casket to fit the tree into.

Hilarious stuff for a pre-adolescent boy. Mrs. Essex and the kids were the same. Great to be around. They were also courageous and honorable people.

Because of distances apart, we don't communicate often but we do stay in touch. Mr. and Mrs. Essex have passed away. The boys, Stuart, Jess and Cooper remain in the funeral home business in Eastern Arkansas and Sarah is a teacher in Texas. They are good people and my life is better because of them.

The Author

David McDonald is retired. He lives in Sherwood, Arkansas. He spends his time in his vegetable garden, piddling with his bee hives, working with recovering alcoholics, and spending time with friends and his large extended family.

Made in the USA
Columbia, SC
16 June 2025

59490014R00109